Precis

Monsters have always been with us—strange beasties that inhabit the night, creatures that defy explanation, myths that suddenly become frighteningly real. Children through the ages have grown up on ghost stories and tales of the "bogeyman." Native religions are filled with devil creatures and other evil apparitions. Half of the world's dreams are nightmares.

Today, mankind is growing up. A number of our old beliefs died hard, but they died. But a belief that has not died is that there are still things out there, going bump in the night, which cannot be easily explained.

And perhaps for good reason . . .

The Authors:

John Lee, Professor of Journalism, has taught at the University of Arizona, New York University and California State University (Long Beach). His books include *Assignation in Algeria, The Killing Wind, Caught in the Act* and *The Ninth Man,* a forthcoming movie.

Barbara Moore, Professor of Journalism at California State University (Northridge), is the author of *Hard on the Road,* a 1974 selection of the Western Writers of America Book Club, and has written for such magazines as *Holiday, Braniff International Magazine* and *Signature.* She is married to John Lee.

Monsters Among Us: Journey to the Unexplained

John Lee and Barbara Moore

PYRAMID BOOKS ▲ NEW YORK

MONSTERS AMONG US: JOURNEY TO THE UNEXPLAINED

A PYRAMID BOOK

Pyramid edition published December, 1975.

ISBN: 0-515-03938-1

Library of Congress Catalog Card Number: 75-27080

Printed in the United States of America

Pyramid Books are published by Pyramid Communications, Inc.
Its trademarks, consisting of the word "Pyramid" and the
portrayal of a pyramid, are registered in the United States
Patent Office.

PYRAMID COMMUNICATIONS, INC.
919 Third Avenue, New York, N.Y. 10022

TABLE OF CONTENTS

Chapter One

TWO ENCOUNTERS

It is a star-kissed night in Murphysboro, Illinois, a hot June evening filled with drifting fireflies and fevered breezes. Gregory A. Cunningham and Jill Anne Thompson are sitting in a parked car at the foot of Twenty-Third Street, on the town's old boat ramp, overlooking the Big Muddy River. The car radio plays softly. Shards of moonlight glitter across the water.

As hot as it is, it is about to get hotter. Jill Thompson is forbidden to date Greg Cunningham. The last thing in the world she needs is to be suddenly propelled into the public eye, where her father will find out about Greg. But that's just what is about to happen.

Meanwhile, bobbing on the surface of Lake Champlain in Vermont, a 15-year-old high school student from Burlington, young Tommy Heinrich, is flycasting from his rowboat.

Lake Champlain, a 107-mile-long slash of water which separates Vermont from the state of New York, is a glacial lake topped by cavernous bluffs, and a haven for fishermen and riverboat excursionists. Naval battles were fought there during the French-Indian War and the War of 1812.

As Tommy flips his spinner across the water, the surface begins to roil and ripple. Something is moving upward toward him.

What do the couple in Murphysboro, Illinois, and the young student on Lake Champlain have in common? They are all about to come face to face with creatures from the unknown, red-blooded American monsters which have been troubling citizens of this

7

country for centuries, just as their shaggy cousins and scaly relatives have been plaguing the rest of the world since time began.

Only it's happening *now*. Today.

Monsters have always been with us—strange beasties that inhabit the night, creatures that defy explanation, myths that suddenly become frighteningly real. Children through the ages have grown up on ghost stories and tales of the "bogeyman." Native religions are filled with devil creatures and other evil apparitions. Half of the world's dreams are nightmares.

Today, mankind is growing up. A number of our old beliefs died hard, but they died. But a belief that has not died is that there are still things out there, going bump in the night, which cannot be easily explained. And perhaps for good reason.

Even now, with the world shrunk to a narrow ball by high-flying jets, with an exploding population which crowds once-isolated areas, with an educated citizenry taught to disregard myths, one can still turn through the pages of the daily newspaper and find stories of strange encounters—creatures that stumble into camping grounds, flickering journeys into the supernatural, dimensions gone crazy, mystifying occurrences, monsters both physical and geographical.

Not all of these reported encounters deserve our attention. Some are products of the imagination, stirred to life by creepy sounds that unleash childhood fears of the dark. Other creatures that men have reported encountering are not monsters at all, but rather perfectly natural by-products of the evolutionary process, frightening only because they are different. Some are hoaxes, because there are always people who seem to enjoy scaring the pants off others. A great many are natural mistakes, the result of poor eyesight or hurried observations or bad light. Some are simply common phenomena, misidentified by shaken witnesses.

8

But some are not so easily explained.

For example, let us return to our couple in the parked car in Murphysboro, Illinois, to see what happens when eyewitness reports are compounded.

It is shortly before midnight on June 25, 1973. Greg Cunningham and Jill Thompson have been talking and listening to the radio. Now, as Jill tries to make up her mind whether or not to go home, they hear something from the woods off to the side of the boat ramp, a sound like an eagle shrieking into a microphone. Greg jerks around, startled. What the heck was that? He flips off the radio and listens.

The sound comes again. A loud, piercing cry. Something is moving through the underbrush, coming into the open. Greg flicks on his headlights. And there it is. A light-colored, hairy creature, about eight-feet tall, looking something like an oversized gorilla. It has long, shaggy, dirty-white hair, matted with mud. It smells foul, like river slime. And it is coming toward the car.

Greg breaks all speed records getting the car started and backing off the boat ramp. He spins around in the street and drives furiously away, muttering to himself. Jill is also frightened.

They drive for a few minutes in semi-silence. Then Greg says, "I think we should tell the police."

"What about my father?" Jill says. "If we talk to the police, he's sure to find out."

Greg shrugs. "It's up to you," he says.

Jill, though she has a lot to lose, is still scared. She decides Greg is right. What they have seen might be dangerous. They must tell the police.

So Greg drives to the police station and makes what is listed as an "unknown creature" report. Soon afterwards, police officers converge down by the river, looking for signs of the creature.

Officer Jimmie Nash is the first to find the footprints, large and peculiar, fast fading away in the oozing mud

9

of the river bank. Officer Nash hadn't been too impressed by the creature report. Like most of us, he has been brought up to believe that monsters are an imaginary product of the past. Only nuts and hysterical old ladies see monsters. Still, Greg Cunningham and Jill Thompson have gone out of their way to report it. They wouldn't have exposed Jill to her father's wrath, and risked ridicule, if they hadn't been really scared.

As Officer Nash bends over the footprints for a closer look, there is a sudden, sharp cry from just a few feet away, and Nash becomes a firm believer. "The most incredible shriek I've ever heard," he is to say later. "It was in those bushes. It was no bobcat or screech owl. We hightailed it out of there."

As soon as Nash and his colleagues reported they had stumbled onto a very queer "something," searchers returned to the area. Police officers searched the woods and the river bank for hours, trying to spot the creature. Every once in a while, they heard odd splashing sounds, like some enormous creature hurrying through knee-deep water. But that was as close as they came.

The next day, the local newspaper, *The Southern Illinoisan,* ran a quiet story on the creature search (it was later covered by *The New York Times*). The couple, Greg Cunningham and Jill Thompson, were not mentioned by name. Murphysboro police assumed that was the end of the story.

It wasn't. The very next night four-year-old Christian Baril was playing in his backyard, trying to catch some elusive fireflies in a glass jar which his mother had given him. Across the fence from him, a big figure rose up in the darkness and stared at him. Christian dropped his jar and hurried back into the house. "Daddy, daddy!" he cried. "There's a big ghost out back!"

A few minutes later, on Cheryl Ray's darkened front porch next door, Cheryl and Randy Creath, the son of a state trooper, were sitting together in the moonlight, talking, when something stirred in the shrubbery near them. Cheryl thought it was some of the kids in the neighborhood, spying on them, and she got up angrily to turn on the porch light. Randy got up too, intending to go out and investigate.

But when the light came on, the two teen-agers were jolted by the same sight that had horrified Greg and Jill the night before—a gigantic, hairy peeping tom, eight feet tall, that smelled like some rotting peat bog.

The teen-agers, speechless, stared at the monster. The monster, in turn, stared at the teen-agers. It seemed an eternity, monster and humans staring at each other from a distance of some 15 feet, but Randy said later that it was probably only about 30 seconds. Then the great shaggy creature turned slowly and shuffled off into the bushes, thrashing his way back toward the river.

The local police chief, Toby Berger, ordered his men out again, all 14 of them, to search for the monster. He even asked a dog trainer in the area, Jerry Nellis, to bring some canine help for the search. Nellis brought his favorite pooch, a big, tough German shepherd named Reb.

While they were searching, officers managed to locate a rough pathway hacked through the underbrush —limbs broken and dangling from bushes, grass trampled underfoot. A trail of black slime led from Cheryl's porch toward the river.

As the officers searched, the German shepherd picked up a scent. He took off at a rush just about where the black slime disappeared and headed off the trail toward the old Bullar farm, an area slightly east of Cheryl Ray's house and north of the river. Officers followed him. But when Reb reached an abandoned barn on the Bullar property, he suddenly yelped and backed away.

11

"What's gotten into Reb?" one of the officers asked.

Nellis, the dog's owner, shook his head in puzzlement. He couldn't understand what had panicked his dog. Reb was known throughout the county for his relentless tracking. But now the dog was acting as if he were some half-witted Chihuahua, instead of an 80-pound German shepherd.

Nellis picked his dog up by the scruff of the neck and thrust him back at the doorway of the barn, trying to get him to go in for a look. The dog dropped to his belly and crawled back, whimpering.

Chief Berger radioed to surrounding communities for help, and an additional dozen police cars responded to his call. But by the time they surrounded the barn and went inside, it was empty.

That was only the beginning. The creature, dubbed the "Murphysboro Monster," continued to haunt the small (population 10,000) Illinois community for weeks through the summer—not only by making appearances, but by its very existence. Townspeople, unexcitable as a rule, began to turn out in force with rifles and shotguns, ready to track the beast down and blow it to bits.

Chief Berger had new problems on his mind now: how to keep his Murphysboro neighbors from shooting each other by accident.

Then, about 10 days later, a traveling carnival came to town and set up shop in Riverside Park, a pleasant green glade on the banks of the Big Muddy, about halfway between the old boat ramp and the sewage treatment plant below Cheryl Ray's house. On July 7, long after the carnival had shut down for the night, three carnival workers named Otis Norris, Wesley Lavander and Ray Adkerson were sitting behind one of the carnival trucks, talking about the day's receipts. A group of carnival ponies, all small and gentle, the kind that are trained to trot docilely around a circle while children sit on their backs, had been tied to bushes on the other side of the truck.

About two o'clock in the morning, the three carnival workers heard a commotion. They got up and walked around the truck to see what was going on. The ponies, far from being gentle, were tugging furiously at their lines. Wide pony eyes rolled in terror as the frightened animals reared and shied.

Puzzled, the three carnival men looked around, wondering what had scared their livestock. Then they saw it. A hairy eight-foot creature, weighing somewhere between 300 and 400 pounds, standing upright in the darkness, calmly watching the ponies.

Creature and men departed the scene simultaneously, each no doubt startling the other in equal measure. The three men went quickly for help, but the creature was long gone when they got back. Temporarily. An hour later, after things quieted down, one of the men summoned to the scene, Charles Kimbal, saw the creature again, peering over the bushes with its head cocked to one side, apparently deeply curious about the ponies.

That was the last official sighting of the Murphysboro creature. The report wasn't lodged immediately. Carnival authorities were afraid news of the extracurricular visitor might hurt business if word got out.

Where did the monster come from? What was it? Where did it go? Chief Berger, still afraid townspeople would shoot each other, went to the town fathers and asked for expert help from outside, someone who could help explain the creature and quiet local fears. The town fathers agreed, and invited Harlan Sorkin from nearby St. Louis, a well-known, serious student of Bigfoot phenomena, to come down for a look.

Sorkin talked to witnesses, went over the grounds of the various sightings, then sifted through the scanty

13

evidence for clues. The descriptions from witnesses all sounded familiar to Sorkin, leading him to what he considered the most likely solution. The Murphysboro visitor was probably from the Shawnee National Forest, a moderate-sized, protected wilderness which straddles Illinois about 400 miles south of Chicago, or some cave down-river from the forest. Ordinarily, Sorkin says, creatures like the Murphysboro visitor are very shy and prefer to remain out of sight, hovering near river bottoms where there is ample vegetation to feed them, but this creature may have been forced out of its home by heavy flooding that occurred that year.

The record book therefore had one more sighting of a probable Bigfoot, one of the shaggy creatures known variously as the Abominable Snowman, or Yeti to natives in the Himalayan Mountains, as Mono Grande in South America, as the Asian Sindai, the Russian Alma, or as Ommo or Sasquatch to American Indians.

Whatever its name, the creature has been popping up with great regularity since populations have been expanding, crowding ever inward on once-isolated pockets where the creatures might have hidden. There have been some 750 reported sightings of such man-like creatures over the past century, more than 300 of them in the last 10 years alone.

Whether the Murphysboro Monster managed to get back to its natural home, no one knows, but at least it seems to have left Murphysboro. The townspeople, generally considered gracious and hospitable, were not at all sorry that this newcomer elected to get out of town.

But what about Tommy Heinrich, whom we left fishing from his boat on Lake Champlain? Is he also about to see a Sasquatch floundering along the shores of the glacial lake? No way. Nor is Tommy's

14

apparition a temporary visitor, forced out of its home by the forces of nature. Tommy's monster is a permanent resident of Lake Champlain, if we are to believe the tales of hundreds of reliable witnesses. And it has been a resident of the lake for more than 300 years. It, or its antecedents.

What is it? Let's stand in the boat behind Tommy and look for ourselves. He has just cast his line toward the middle of the lake when he sees the water begin to swirl. Tommy is a gutty lad, and he doesn't drop his rod and start rowing for shore the second he spots movement, even though he has heard the stories. Rather, he sits numbly and stares at the surface of the water, waiting to see what appears.

The dark waters part briefly, and a snakelike body, gray or rust-colored, rises. Water streams down its back. Though it's hard to tell as the creature wriggles to the surface, it is somewhere between 20- and 45-feet long. Then Tommy catches sight of its head. A long-snouted face, shaped something like a horse's head. Two small horns, or what appear to be horns, sprout from the forehead. It doesn't stay long. Its eyes sweep around and catch sight of Tommy and it ducks instantly, plunging back into the depths. The whole encounter takes just a few seconds.

Now Tommy drops his rod and starts rowing. And who can blame him?

Tommy Heinrich saw the creature in 1969. He is now a young man, old enough to vote, and old enough to think twice before waiting if he ever sees it again. "I don't know what it was," he says. "Maybe a monster, maybe a weird fish. But I can tell you one thing. Something peculiar, something very definitely strange, lives out there."

Tommy is only one of hundreds who have seen something cavorting in the waters of Lake Champlain. Whatever it is, witnesses claim it travels "in high gear," moving across the quiet waters in serpentine fashion. Many of the witnesses through the decades have been thoroughly reputable people. They include a county sheriff, a school principal and a newspaper publisher, as well as large groups of people on riverboat steamers, on shoreside picnics and even at a bridge-opening ceremony in 1945.

Skeptics, and there are many among the 200,000 residents of the area, claim that monsters are only in the eye of the beholder, that old stories of sea serpents and snaky creatures from the deep have led excited witnesses to see monsters where none exist. It's just a large fish, they say. Or a log bobbing on the surface of the water.

Whatever it is, it may have been there as long as the lake itself. The Indians may have been the first to see it, since they were the first in the area. But the oldest recorded sighting of the Lake Champlain monster took place, fittingly, in 1609, when the French explorer Samuel de Champlain, for whom the lake was named, discovered the inland strip of water and wrote down his impressions of a serpent-like creature whose body was as thick as a wine cask.

Then came the inland sea battles of the French-Indian War and the War of 1812. The Lake Champlain creature was smart enough to stay low while the grapeshot was flying. Some of those old gunners were notoriously inaccurate.

The creature was next spotted in 1819, then disappeared until more and more people began to settle the area. During the 30-year period between 1870 and 1900, there were enough sightings to set off a full-scale monster scare. It was during this period that the sheriff, N. H. Mooney, and the newspaper publisher, Wendell Lansing of the *Essex County Republican,* joined the list of witnesses.

Nor have all the witnesses been solitary people,

alone on the shores of the lake. Groups have been treated to swimming displays on at least six occasions. The first group encounter came in 1871, when a number of passengers aboard the steamer *Curlew* looked out across the waters and saw the beastie splashing past them about 40 feet away. Then, in 1892, members of the American Canoe Association, on their annual outing, saw the monster rise up right in the middle of a flotilla of canoes, scattering them in every direction.

More recently, passengers aboard the *S. S. Ticonderoga,* watching a bridge-opening ceremony in 1945 from the center of the lake, saw the creature's head rise out of the water, almost as if curious to see what all the fuss was about. That same year, a couple from Rouse's Point, New York, were out in a rowboat for an afternoon outing when the creature surfaced near enough for them to "whack it with an oar." More prudent, the couple departed the lake instantly, and for days following the harrowing experience, the woman was sick in bed.

Then, in 1954, a high school principal with three fishing companions spotted it splashing about their fishing camp. Ten years later, in 1965, it was kids at a summer camp. They were taking a swimming break when the creature popped up and did some swimming of its own. Camp counselors reported they had difficulty getting the kids even to go close to the water after that.

But the creature supposedly isn't dangerous. The *Burlington Free Press,* reporting on the sightings in a news story, pooh-poohed accounts of those who claim the monster has bad breath and breathes sulphur flames. The newspaper claimed rather that the monster has grown toothless, gentle and tame over the years. "Oftentimes," the paper said, "the white gulls, his friends, rest upon his back."

Are such creatures as the Murphysboro and Lake Champlain monsters real? Or are they simply optical mistakes made by honest, well-meaning folks?

That is what we're going to try to determine in this book.

Chapter Two

MONSTERS AMONG US

All manner of horrors lurked in the darkness outside early man's cave. Monsters gripped his psyche. That which could not be explained grew out of proportion to that which could. Fears became stories, and stories became legend, and legend became truth, duly reported and repeated from parent to child down through the ages, growing larger and more horrible with each succeeding generation.

By the time the Middle Ages rolled around, there was a veritable mythological zoo surrounding the cave dweller's narrow world. A zoo peopled with dragons and minotaurs and unicorns, with griffins and tatzel-wurms and sciapodes, with phoenixes and chimeras and spinxes, all writhing and rambling through the borders of man's consciousness, breathing fire, roaring in anger, killing, mystifying, then vanishing with a wave of the tail.

People knew everything they wanted to know about monsters—how they lived, what they ate, what they looked like. They might never have seen one in the flesh, but they had heard the stories. They knew, for example, that monsters have monstrous habits, were evil, promiscuous and dirty. They had a bad smell, often like sulphur and brimstone, and they were usually allied with the Devil. They ate all manner of vile things:

18

rats, mice, lizards, flies, dogs, snails, cats and, more often than not, people. Occasionally they ate their own parents or even their children, which was a good idea; otherwise the world population of monsters might well have gotten out of hand.

An example of these early mythical beasts which darkened man's horizons was a ghastly creature known as the basilisk, a horror so vile that its breath could wilt trees and shatter boulders. A winged reptile, which legend tells us was born of an egg laid by a rooster and hatched by snakes in the warmth of a dungheap, the basilisk was never seen by anyone who lived to tell about it (which can only make one wonder how its story first surfaced), because all living creatures, humans included, automatically dropped dead at the sight of it. The one exception to this rule was the lowly weasel. Since the weasel was immune to the basilisk's horrible looks, people who had been terrorized by the beasts usually tied mirrors to weasels and sent them in to face the basilisk. The basilisk took one look at itself in the weasel-propelled mirror and promptly died of self-induced horror. Thanks heavens there were only a few rooster eggs to worry about.

The basilisk legend was fairly short-lived. Other mythological monsters were allowed to live longer, especially the gentlest, most charming of the creatures —the ubiquitous unicorns. Unicorns, fabulous four-footed beasts with long, single horns jutting from the middle of their foreheads, were reputedly seen many times in various parts of the world. The mother of Confucius saw one. Herodotus saw one. So did Pliny, even to describing its remarkable ability to evade hunters by somersaulting over cliffs. The unicorn was nice to have around. Its horn changed color in the presence of poison, and so it was invaluable to kings in fear of their lives. Further, its horn, when powdered, could ward off a remarkable array of diseases. As a matter of fact, it was possible to get some powdered unicorn horn at almost any of the corner alchemists in the old days.

The unicorn had a rich, satisfying life, lasting almost 4,000 years before he became a victim of science. In 1665, when plague victims turned to the dust of unicorn horns to save them, the powder failed. People were so disappointed that they almost stopped believing in the creature. By 1746, the unicorn horn had finally been dropped from the list of required pharmaceutical drugs kept by the Royal Society of Physicians in London.

Dragons are another hardy mythical beast with a long lifeline. Huge, fire-breathing reptiles, dragons were usually in league with the evil forces in the universe. They had a dietary fondness for fair young maidens, which may be why so many knights in shining armor were always out trying to hunt them down. The quickest way to become a hero in those dragon days of yore was to slay one.

Then there were the medieval griffins, creatures with the head and wings of an eagle and the body of the lion, and earlier half-and-half beasts such as the minotaur and the centaur. The minotaur was a lone monster with the head of a bull and the body of a man, confined in a labyrinth on the isle of Minos. He was fed a yearly tribute of seven young men and seven young women, a feast he gobbled up gratefully. The centaur, on the other hand, was a race of beasts, not a single mistake of nature. Half-man, half-horse, centaurs were considered savage and quite uncouth.

The half-and-half horrors inevitably led to the addition of a more appealing half-and-half creature—the mermaid. Mermaids, sea-dwelling creatures with the head and body of a woman and a fishtail where the legs should be, were apparently always very beautiful (whoever heard of an ugly mermaid?) and possessed great charm, but they used the charm to lure sea-faring men to their deaths. For what it's worth, there were also mermen, but few writers ever bothered to waste ink on them.

The beasts of mythology took many shapes, and the list of them could fill an entire book (and has, several times). But the beginnings of a new art called science finally came along and knocked the underpinnings from beneath most of them. It was hard to believe in such creatures when scientists told us they weren't possible. Of course those same early scientists told us flight wasn't possible, that the world was flat, that the earth was the center of the universe, and so forth. But they seemed to know what they were talking about, and mythological monsters gradually faded from the list of things to fear.

Consider the poor dragon. In 1572, an Italian farmer saw a dragon crossing the road on two feet. It was only about three feet long, and was apparently quite young, since its fire-breathing apparatus wasn't functioning. The farmer promptly killed it with his hoe. Then he dragged it off to town to show the authorities. A leading zoologist of the time took one look at it and declared it to be an animal "such as had never been seen before in all Europe, namely a dragon with two feet." But other contemporary scientists said no, hold on. Just because there was a body in evidence didn't mean that dragons were real creatures after all. Their main objection? The creature had only two feet, therefore it wasn't a dragon. It was only a monstrosity.

The first "reasonable" scientific definition of monsters came in the Eighteenth Century when Linnaeus (Carl von Linné) put together his famous classification of all living things. He included a remarkable category which he dubbed *Homo monstrosus.* It was a large category, related to *Homo sapiens,* but quite different in appearance. Linnaeus had never really seen any of these

21

semi-human species, but he had centuries of literature on which to base his descriptions. They came in a variety of grotesque shapes—people with pointy heads, people with tiny heads, people with bulging heads, with dog heads, with monkey heads, fish scales, hairy creatures, men and women with feathers. He had read about them all in the journals of leading explorers and traveling diaryists. We can still see versions of Linnaeus's catalogue on colorful posters outside the freak shows at most circuses and carnivals.

Although the budding discipline of science helped man begin to weed out his mythological monsters, leaving only freaks, it failed to foresee the inevitable—that man would invent new and hardier beasts to people his darker hours. The new monsters were killers—mysterious, vicious, tainted with superstition, often blood-sucking denizens of the undead. And nearly always taking the shape of man himself.

Compare the average Renaissance man, whose knowledge was so meager, with Twentieth-Century man. During the 1973 UFO hubbub that will be considered in Chapter Eight, there was an outbreak of mysterious animal deaths in the Midwest, such as has occurred at other times and elsewhere—in England and in Sweden, for example. Cows, horses and dogs were found dead, often with their throats cut with surgical-like precision. As the *Kansas City Times* reported of cattle deaths on December 22, 1973, "Two points confounding investigators have been the absence of blood and footprints. Even on warm days, with the carcass freshly killed, there has been no bleeding on or around the animal. Some believe the cattle were drained of blood. No human tracks have been detected near each mutilation, even in fresh snow."

The coincidental report of numerous UFO sightings led many otherwise calm people to speculate that creatures from outer space had some need for animal blood

—and perhaps that of humans. Consider what the poor Renaissance man, his mind clouded with super-stition, thought as he walked alone on a dark night, perhaps passing the village cemetery, nervously eyeing a blood-red moon overhead with heavy, macabre clouds scudding before a cold wind.

Even if his area had not been plagued with phantom animal killers, the slightest sound could send him fleeing for his life. For out there, in the black borders of his subconscious, lived the new terrors. There were vam-pires, sleeping in coffins by day, drinking the blood of innocents by night. There were werewolves, pos-sessed by demons and sent into a raging insanity every time the full moon came out. There were ghouls, bloody horrors which robbed graves of the newly dead and fed on corpses. In other parts of the world, there were zombies, corpses themselves, who walked around in a catatonic state doing the bidding of some evil master. There were ghosts, witches, hobgoblins, dark and loath-some fiends which prowled the night. Is it any wonder that Renaissance man whistled loudly to buttress his courage?

But the early scientists who had taken such a hard line on the two-footed dragon had been on the right track, and the reaction to this shift in monster emphasis was a hardened approach to monster labeling. It wasn't enough to "see" a monster anymore. Never mind that villages shut down with the setting of the sun and no one in his right mind would venture out; the new science insisted that a beast be captured and examined before it could be accepted. If you couldn't lead scien-tists to a vampire or a werewolf stuffed away in a cage somewhere, waiting for them to pull out their calipers and flasks and boiling vats for a little controlled investi-gation, then no such creature existed.

Not that this budding scientific approach always worked. An Englishman named Andrew Battell, who lived in Africa in the Seventeenth Century was said to have witnessed a very strange creature, "a kinde of Great Apes, if they might be so termed, of the height of a man but twice as bigge in features of their limmes with strength proportionable, hairie all over, otherwise altogether like men and women in the whole bodily shape." Scientists scoffed at the notion. Sheer fantasy, they insisted. Show us one, they said. If you can't show us one, it doesn't exist. And it remained fantasy for 200 years, until gorillas were finally "officially" discovered.

The gorilla is only one of many "mythical creatures" which were tardy in joining the scientist's realm of reality. There are others. The Komodo lizard, which some think may be a version of the earlier dragon, the giant panda, the pygmy hippopotamus, the snub-nosed langur—all have been discovered in the last 150 years. Imagine the derision that must have been heaped on the first person to describe the duck-billed platypus, an egg-laying mammal with a muzzle shaped like a duck's bill, furry, but with webbed feet.

Like rare animals, modern monsters seem to prefer privacy. They are said to live in the rugged terrain of uninhabited Asian mountains, or in the untamed wildernesses (shrinking all the time) of the American Rockies and coastal ranges, or in the depths of Scotland's Loch Ness.

And, keeping pace with our burgeoning technology, an even newer breed of monsters has developed. Ufology and science fiction have given us visitors from outer space, the well-known BEMs (Bug-Eyed Monsters) and MIBs (Men in Black), little green men in silver space suits, and creatures with bullet-shaped heads and crab claws for hands. Or, if you prefer, there are godlike humanoid creatures from outer space who look like us, only handsomer, smarter, and loaded with enough super-sophisticated technology to make our precision instruments look like gaudy pinball machines.

Nor do all monsters of today take human or animal form. There are what may be called geographical monsters like the Bermuda Triangle or the Ring of Fire or the Devil's Sea, off Japan. There are also reports of monsters which inhabit the mind, such as demons and devils, defying exorcism. There are inexplicable mental powers, such as ESP and telepathy.

Modern science, unlike the stiff-backed science of old, doesn't profess to have all the answers. Proving that something does *not* exist is very difficult, if not logically impossible, and until and unless indisputable proof of the existence of modern monsters appears, everyone must decide the questions for himself.

But the pursuit of evidence may not take long. The world is closing in on our last strongholds of isolation, and the monsters, if they exist, will soon have no hiding place left untouched by the mainstream of civilization.

Take the example of one of the most persistently evasive of modern monsters—a humanlike creature which supposedly chose as its home perhaps the most inaccessible spot on earth, the heights of the Himalaya mountains. Safe for centuries, it was only a whisper around Sherpa campfires, tales of giant footprints seen in snow and ice, unexpected droppings by outcroppings of rocks, or a mere shadowy figure on a high horizon, glimpsed from time to time by travelers through a snowy pass. Had the Himalayas remained inaccessible, reports of the creature might never have come to the public's attention. But nothing remains untouched in a shrinking world. Time crowded in even on the Himalayas.

And gave us the Abominable Snowman.

Chapter Three

THE ABOMINABLE SNOWMAN

It was sunset. In the distance, the long sweep of crystal peaks flushed red. Even before the sirdar (head porter) gave the command, Tashi dropped his heavy pack and turned to stare with familiar awe and admiration.

The "Himalayas," that was what the European sahib called the mountains. Poor sahib. He didn't know any of the right names. He even appeared to think sacred Chomolungma, "the mountain over which no bird can fly," was something called Everest. Tashi privately throught the elder porters ought to tell the sahib the truth, but they never paid any attention to what Tashi thought. Tashi was only 17.

"Toi ye!" was the only thing the sirdar ever said to him. "Climb!"

And climb Tashi had, up the glaciers, along the moraines. He'd lost track of the days, but then days didn't matter. They were somewhere in northeastern Sikkim, preparing to make camp in the snow at 17,000 feet, and even though the work was hard, Tashi was enjoying himself thoroughly. This was why he had left home—to see the great world.

Not that he didn't love his home, too. Home was good, especially when his father sent him out with the yaks to wander, free and alone, even higher than they were now, under the walls of the great mountains.

Tashi didn't daydream of home long. The sirdar snapped commands that began the evening routine of pitching the sahib's tent and making a tiny fire to brew his tea. After walking all day, the sahib, naturally, took a walk, and Tashi grinned to himself as he went about his work. He'd never met a sahib before, and he had to wonder if they were all so odd. This one, from someplace called England, was a major in something called the Indian Army Medical Corps. The word around the camp was that he was going to write a book about Tashi's mountains. Tashi knew what books were. He'd seen one once, a rare thing, in a monastery, and he was very impressed with the sahib.

But he was less impressed a few minutes later. The sahib came rushing back to camp with that long-legged stride of his and spoke to the sirdar, and they both turned and hurried back the way the sahib had come. A porter named Dawa had been within earshot. Rumor ran quickly around the camp.

No one had said they couldn't follow the sahib, and they all did. Then, beyond a small icefall, they saw what had excited him so much: Disappearing into the distance along the edge of a glacier, a line of huge, humanlike footprints was impressed in the snow.

Tashi shivered, and not from the cold. Up in the high places with his father's yaks, he had seen such tracks before. Probably most of the men here had seen them. As always, the tracks frightened Tashi a little, but he regarded them with curiosity, too. He listened as the sahib asked the sirdar in the halting Tibetan in which they communicated, "But what could have made them?" The sirdar shook his head in stubborn ignorance.

"You men," the sahib called. "Does someone know these tracks? Are they bear? Snow-bear?"

No one answered. The sahib looked angry. He put his booted foot in one of the tracks. The sahib had big feet himself, much bigger than Tashi's, but the track in the snow was twice as broad and almost twice as long.

The men shifted uneasily, and Tashi could stand

their silence no longer. Poor sahib, they never told him anything. "Yeti, sahib," he burst out. He pointed at the enormous track that looked like a bare human footprint in the snow, if humans came eight or nine feet tall and had a habit of walking around barefoot in the snows of the world's most isolated mountain range. "Yeti!"

The year was 1889, and if to a 17-year-old porter the strange footprints had an obvious explanation, to Major W. A. Waddell, doctor of law, fellow of the Linnaean Society, they were far more mystifying.

When Waddell returned to civilization and wrote his book, *Among the Himalayas,* he cautiously wrote of the footprints, "These were alleged to be the trail of the hairy wild men who are believed to live amongst the eternal snows."

In 1921, a new and far more fascinating bit of terminology was born for the curious to chew on. Then, leading the first expedition to reconnoiter a possible way to climb Mount Everest, Lieutenant-Colonel C. K. Howard-Bury looked down far below to the valleys of the Lhapta Pass to see what appeared to be great, dark, unclothed, hairy but human forms walking slowly across the snows.

He was assured by the porters that the creatures were members of the species they called *Metohkangmi* —the Abominable Snowman.

Thus, with a set of tracks, a brief sighting and a collection of names, onto the stage of the Western world strode the creature that would baffle it to the present decade. Mysterious footprints would be spotted many times, and even photographed. Folklore and supposed "scalps" of the Snowman would be examined. Mountaineers, newspapermen and a Texas oilman would strike out into the Himalayas on repeated expeditions, seeking some final proof of its existence, but without success. In the eighty years following Waddell's first sighting, only two Europeans ever laid eyes on what conceivably might be an Abominable Snowman, and then only momentarily and in poor light.

But if to Europeans the Abominable Snowman, or Yeti, remains an elusive target in a game of anthropological hide-and-seek, to native dwellers of the massive snow kingdom of the Himalayas it is so familiar that the Nepalese, for example, subdivide the Yeti into two distinct subtypes, the vicious *Dzu-teh,* a hairy specimen eight feet tall or taller, and the smaller, shyer *Meh-teh.*

Both are familiar bogeymen of childhood. "Hish, hish, the Yeti will get you," the young porter Tashi had been told since babyhood when his playing got too rowdy. Another young porter from the high Himalayas who went on to become one of the most famous men in the world had also heard plenty of Yeti stories, not the least riveting of which was the time his father met one face to face.

The boy grew up to be Tenzing Norgay, a sturdy little Sherpa who at 11:30 in the morning of May 29, 1953, climbed the final 30 feet to the top of Mount Everest with Sir Edmund Hillary and became co-conquerer of the world's highest mountain.

The sun was shining that morning and the sky was the deepest blue Tenzing had ever seen. They stood on the summit of the world for about 15 minutes. Tenzing looked down. All the rest of the world was under him. Nuptse to the west. Lhotse to the south. Makalu to the east. But dearer to him even than these great mountaintops was the far, faint jumble of the old Thyangoche monastery. Beyond Thyangoche were the valleys and villages of Solo Khumbu—his home.

Solo Khumbu was full of stories about the Abominable Snowman. The "Tiger of the Snows," as the world dubbed Tenzing after he safely climbed down from the

29

mountain, never himself saw a Yeti, but as a boy up on the stone-slopes and glaciers, he had sometimes found a strange animal's droppings, containing traces of rats and worms, and he was certain it could only be evidence that a Yeti had been there.

Before Tenzing was born, the story went, his father had even come upon one suddenly on the Barun Glacier.

Neither party desired the meeting, Ghang La Mingma would solemnly tell the children when they begged to hear the tale again. Then he would begin: "Before I knew what was happening, it was so close that I saw it clearly."

"What did it look like, father?" Tenzing's sister, Lahmu Kipa, invariably asked.

"It looked like a big monkey or ape, except that its eyes were deeply sunken and its head was pointed at the top. The color was grayish, and a noticeable thing was that the hair grew in two directions—from above the waist upward and from below the waist downward. It was about four feet high, and a female."

"Did it run, father?" Lahmu Kipa would prompt.

"Did it run! We both ran. We both were frightened. Right away it turned and began climbing a steep mountain slope, making a high, shrill whistle, and soon it had disappeared."

Tenzing's father was worried, of course. Many people claimed that if a man saw a Yeti, he would surely die. Fortunately for the family, the curse did not work with full effectiveness on Ghang La Mingma, and he was only very sick afterwards, for almost a year.

Then, in 1935, when the proud father had gone to visit his son on Tenzing's first Everest expedition, lightning struck twice and he saw the second Yeti of his lifetime.

The first Tenzing knew about it was when Ghang La Mingma arrived, breathless from a hasty climb, at

Camp Two, where Tenzing was relaying supplies to the higher camps. Ghang La Mingma had spent the night alone in Camp One on a glacier, while everyone else was either down below at the base camp or up higher on the mountain. He looked shaken as he rushed to embrace Tenzing.

"I come all this way to see my son," he panted. "And instead what I see is a Yeti!"

Tenzing turned pale under his dark mountaineer's sunburn. There was no *chang,* the strong Sherpa beer, but he hurriedly made his father tea to give him strength before asking for his story.

It had happened at dawn. In the great silence of the mountain, a man alone is keenly conscious of any sound, and Ghang La Mingma bolted upright in his blankets at the first note of a queer, high whistling sound outside his tent.

He feared what he had to do next, but he had to do it. He had to know. Fumbling for his felt boots, he raised the tent flap and looked out. There was a creature a little way off, coming down the glacier from south to north.

Ghang La Mingma felt his bones turn to icy jelly. What to do? Run? But no, it would see him. Great Buddha, it might chase him!

Then hide in the tent—maybe it wouldn't see him. But . . . but if it *didn't* see him, what if it came nearer? What if . . . what if it even came into the tent?

Ghang La Mingma averted his eyes. He didn't want to look at the Yeti. He forced himself to stay exactly where he was, head visible outside the raised tent flap, trying by this method to warn the Yeti that a human was present.

"Then it went on down the glacier and was out of sight, and I came up to you as fast as I could!" Ghang La Mingma finished in a rush. "It didn't hurt me. *Thuji chey.* I am grateful."

31

No evil befell Tenzing's father afterwards. He didn't even get sick—according to Tenzing, because his father hadn't seen this last Yeti as closely.

Since Tenzing spent most of his adult life climbing in isolated country, it was almost inevitable that he would run into traces of the Abominable Snowman himself. In his excellent autobiography of an adventurous life, *Tiger of the Snows,* co-written with James Ramsey Ullman, Tenzing relates that he twice saw tracks. But he never saw a Yeti in the flesh, and he never wished to see one.

Did a lifetime spent in the area supposedly haunted by the Yeti cause him to believe that they really existed? Let him tell you in his own words:

"I am not a superstitious man. I do not believe the Yeti is anything supernatural, nor do I believe many of the crazy stories I have heard. But I do not think my father was a liar and made his stories up out of his head. And certainly the tracks I have seen both on the Zemu Glacier in 1946 and near Everest in 1952 do not look like those of any familiar creature. Though I cannot prove it, I am convinced that some such thing exists."

Tenzing arrived at the conclusion that the Abominable Snowman is not a man but an animal that moves around mostly at night and lives on the plants and smaller animals of the highest mountain pastures, maybe an ape of a type as yet unknown to us.

Of the expeditions that have gone searching unsuccessfully for the Abominable Snowman, he mused, "Though this was disappointing it was also perhaps just as well. We now go to so many places, do so much, find out so much. I think it is all right if there are still a few things we do not know."

Chapter Four

TRACKING THE AMERICAN BIGFOOT

Has America its own version of the Abominable Snowman?

Ask any of the 13 teen-age boys who were present during certain memorable nights in Oregon, and you'll get 13 loud shouts of "Yes!"

Many scientists, on the other hand, flatly say "No." Others are merely profoundly skeptical. A few are at least willing to consider the idea. But the group of teenagers in Oregon think they know for certain. They saw it. They hunted it. One thinks he shot it twice with a 12-gauge shotgun. Three think that *it* hunted *them!*

The track record of the mysterious beast is far more complete on the American continent than in Asia. Stories of the Sasquatch, or Oh-mah'ah, or Omah, or Ommo, have been part of American Indian tradition for centuries. And ever since 1811, when an American explorer first reported having found giant, humanlike footprints, the creature now most commonly called Bigfoot has been leaving hundreds of footprints, occasional rough "beds" of grass or boughs, a horrible stench and terrified citizens in its wake.

In the Nineteenth Century, newspaper accounts of "Wild Hairy Men" turned up from Arkansas to California, where Gold Rush miners supposedly had numerous encounters with huge, manlike beasts, or, contrarily, beastlike men. Today, although reports come in from as far afield as Montana, Idaho, Missouri, Illinois, West Virginia, Michigan, Nebraska and Texas, most Bigfoot sightings are in the rugged Pacific Northwest, in mountainous Northern California, Washington, Oregon and the environs of British Columbia.

It was high up the Bluff Creek Valley in Northern California that a Bigfoot hunter named Roger Patterson succeeded in shooting a few controversial feet of fuzzy movie film of what he swore was a female Bigfoot in the fall of 1967. It was a year later in the little city of The Dalles, Oregon, that Patterson tracked down the group of boys who had spent a few nights in June, 1967 in one of the wildest monster hunts on record.

None of the boys was over 18. They had been carrying guns and staying up until all hours, and so their hunt did not receive the warmest possible approval of either their parents or the law. Their names have been changed, at their request, but here are the facts as they saw them:

There was more than one Bigfoot. The creatures left footprints, of which the boys took photographs, that ranged in length from 19 to 23½ inches. The creature's dimensions were roughly from eight to 10 feet tall, and they guessed its weight at about 450 pounds.

All told, it was quite a sight to run up on suddenly, the night Doug Sealy and Bruce Williams first discovered the world might contain a huge creature named Bigfoot.

They'd been out fooling around, the way kids sometimes get the urge to do when it's June. They were walking along a winding road coming from the golf course, and up on a bluff above the road some kids were apparently following them. Doug and Bruce could tell, especially when loose rocks rolled down from the bluff.

"Let's hide down the bank," Doug said. "We'll teach 'em to roll rocks on us. When they come down to the road looking for us, we'll rush up and scare 'em."

The plan sounded okay to Bruce. He figured their followers were some kids from a nearby trailer court, or maybe some of the other guys who apparently were sleeping out that night. He was sure of it seconds later. As Bruce and Doug hunkered in their hiding place, they could hear rocks clicking and brush rustling heavily as if the kids had started pell-mell down the bluff. He punched Doug and started up to confront them.

"Wait!" Doug said suddenly. "Oh good Lord, what *is* that?"

Bruce sucked in his breath, spotting it at the same instant. "There aren't any kids around here that size," he said. "Let's get out of here!"

With unspoken agreement, they clambered over a fence and ran across a field, heading for the distant freeway. But before they got more than 70 yards into the field Doug gasped. "It's following us! Did you see that? It went through the fence! It just went right through, like it wasn't even there!"

The two boys stopped running, and when they stopped so did the huge, shadowy creature. It was standing on two feet, and it appeared to be watching them.

The rest of the trip to the freeway was a nightmare they'll never forget. When the boys ran, the creature would run. If they stopped, it stopped. If they'd walk, it would walk. But its steps were about three times as long as theirs, and the creature was catching up with them.

They made a last, frantic dash to the freeway, and there, at last, the creature stopped following them. They stood, breathing hard, trying to figure out where it had gone, and got another shock when a car came around the curve. In the headlights coming toward them, they saw the creature crossing the freeway in back of them.

"It's trying to sneak up on us," Bruce said nervously.

"No, maybe not," Doug said, trying to sound reassuring. "Maybe he just didn't know anything about us and was just going to the river or something."

They caught a ride into town, but they were too excited even to think about sleep, and too curious to let the matter drop there. By first light, about four or five in the morning, they had returned with some other boys in a car, to see what the creature might be in daylight. Right where it had come down the bank after them, they saw it coming up. They screeched the car to a stop.

"Let's chase it!" said Nat Heller, one of the new boys. "I got a knife."

"You're outta your mind," Doug said. "What are you going to do, whittle it to death with a pocketknife?"

"Well, then, we'll stone him to death. Come on!"

With more courage than good sense, the boys took out after the creature. A shocked little city named The Dalles, Oregon, might have been planning a mass funeral that day, except for the fortunate fact that the boys were unable to get close to the creature. It easily outdistanced them and left them behind.

Doug and Bruce didn't get much of a chance to catch up on their sleep that day. Rumors of what they had seen swept from friend to friend, and they were kept busy repeating the creature's description. Its body was covered with dark, red-brown hair. Except that its eyes glowed red in reflected light, like an animal's, it looked more human than anything else. A lot of the boys said, aw, they'd just seen a bear, but Doug argued about that.

"We rule out bears," he said. "We rule them out in the first place because bears don't walk on their back legs and don't run on their back legs and whatever this is did."

Then, to an excited newcomer, he added, "It smelled rancid, like somebody who hasn't taken a bath for maybe two or three years."

"Yeah, but what do you mean, rancid?" pressed the 13-year-old brother of one of his chums. "Exactly what did it smell like?"

36

"Well, it just smelled terrible. I don't know if I ever smelled anything that smelled like it before, so I wouldn't know exactly what it smelled like. It smelled like maybe a cow that's been dead and mouldy for a couple of months, that's about what it smelled like. Terrible."

The group of boys concluded that since there were numerous caves in the hilly area above the road, maybe the creature—or creatures—slept in one during the day and, like a nocturnal animal that feeds and drinks mainly at night, headed at nighttime for the river, through the cut in which they now had twice spotted it.

So that night, Doug, Bruce and 11 other boys embarked on a full-fledged Bigfoot hunt. No pocketknives or stones this time. Everybody brought what guns they could get hold of—a few .22s, and also .270s and 30.06s and a 7mm and a 6.5mm, and one kid named Davy Crammer brought a 12-gauge shotgun with "00" buckshot.

They were all scared to death, but they weren't about to let that stop them. They were even disappointed when, the first night of their formal hunt, they only saw a creature at too great a distance to shoot at. The second night, the boys were there again. They were luckier—or, depending on how you look at it, unluckier—because this time they saw two creatures go straight through the cut, then turn right.

It was dark. It was late at night. It took nerve, but Doug Sealy and Davy Crammer decided to take Davy's 12-gauge and go down to see if they could spot where the creatures had gone.

Not unexpectedly, it was too dark to do any tracking, and they were walking back up to join the other boys when they walked by a big shadowy fir tree growing on the slope.

"Listen," Davy said, "we'd better check that tree. What if they're hiding in the branches?"

On the uphill side of the tree, branches came all the way to the ground. Doug wasn't too keen about getting very close to it, but he reached down and pulled up a branch.

They saw it. It was no further than 10 feet away from them. Well, maybe a little farther, but the boys were too startled to be fussy about measurements. There was only one creature, but that was plenty. Although it was crouching, even in a crouched position it looked at least seven feet tall, and when it raised to its full height, you could add two full feet to that.

Davy, standing to Doug's right, shot so fast that he didn't even raise the shotgun to his shoulder. He shot from the hip, twice, and the monstrous shape on the other side of the tree went down. It began to roll away from them down the steep bank.

"We got it!" Davy shouted.

"Where'd it go?"

"It just rolled, and when it stops rolling it's gonna be there, dead. C'mon!"

They rushed down the bank after the creature. But immediately, it was back up on its feet. It ran. Like the first time Doug had seen the creature, it went right through a fence, this one of four-strand barbed wire, snapping off three big wooden fence poles flush with the ground.

Halting their wild plunge down the bank, Doug and Davy looked after the creature indecisively.

"It's not hurt as bad as we thought," Doug said.

Davy nodded. "I only got one more shot. I don't think . . ."

"Naw, we'd better not go after him. We'd better get back to the other guys and warn them. He's wounded. He's more than likely gonna be mad."

"Yeah. Listen, we'd better all get back to town and let him cool off. We can come back when it's day-time and track him. He'll run until he can't run anymore, you know, like a wounded deer or something. Then we'll find him dead."

They didn't. Oh, there was blood when they came back at noon, and tracks that the boys photographed, but after maybe a hundred yards the tracks petered out and there wasn't enough blood for the boys to be able to follow.

Many of the boys figured it was time to give up monster hunting. Some came back several more times. They heard what they thought were creatures, clattering through the rocks of the cut, and they would hastily position themselves to try to get the creatures in a cross-fire. If they failed in shooting themselves, it was probably because the creatures only put in distant appearances. Once there was one, sometimes two, once as many as three.

The final night of their hunt dampened all the young hunters' zeal. The group had dwindled to five boys, and they split up into two teams.

Ricky Harrison went with the three-man team. He had the only gun among them, a light little .22. He thought the last night of his young life had come when the trio of hunters heard a rock click right in back of them.

The boys whirled. Eight feet behind them, one of the giant creatures whirled, too. It had been following them, and now it ran.

"Shoot, Ricky!" one of the other boys yelped.

"Shut up!" Ricky said. "He's leaving."

And that, for Ricky, was that. A .22 was not enough gun for a nine- or 10-foot monster. Maybe an elephant gun wouldn't have been enough gun. The creature was leaving, and Ricky figured he'd just as soon let him leave.

The boys never went back for another night of monster-hunting. There were other things to do on June nights, girls to date, sodas to drink, cars to ride around in. They had seen their monsters. They had measured their foot-and-a-half long, eight- or 10-inch-wide footprints. They had their memories. In soft summer rains, the footprints faded. The memories never will.

The attitude of most people who have seen—or thought they've seen—a living Bigfoot has been nicely summed up by Clayton Mack, a hunting guide intimate with the wilds of British Columbia. As he told former newspaper publisher John Green *(Agassiz-Harrison Advance)*, after seeing a massive, humanlike figure on an isolated island, "I heard about these Sasquatches ever since I was a kid, but I just didn't believe in them, you know. But now I've been thinking I believe it."

Many serious anthropologists and zoologists, however, would require more than even the evidence of their own eyes to consider seriously the possibility there is such a thing as an Abominable Snowman or a Bigfoot.

Where, they ask, is the hard evidence that other scientists could examine—the skulls, the skeletons, the captive animals? Where are even the unquestionably valid photographs or movie films of such creatures?

"In the fall, the hunters are out there killing everything," the curator of primatology at the Smithsonian Institution, Dr. Richard Thorington, has pointed out gently. "It's highly unlikely that you wouldn't bring some of them in."

Most physical anthropologists would at least like to see a logical and continuous evolutionary line from the family tree of man and ape, and other such evidence as the existence of a breeding population large enough to escape extinction, before they will do more than quietly shake their hands.

Such scientists consider probabilities when they probe data, and when probabilities get too low they think the limited time and money available to science are better devoted elsewhere. Yet, as a purely personal pastime, scientists find speculating about monsters as intriguing as the next person, and a few have devoted systematic study to the "soft evidence"—such as eyewitness reports and footprints—of the Bigfoot/Abominable Snowman phenomenon.

One Belgian zoologist, Dr. Bernard Heuvelmans, has gone on record stating the Abominable Snowman is a descendant of an early creature that preceded the development of mankind, *Gigantopithecus,* some of whose giant teeth and two jawbones have been found in northern India in the Siwalik Hills, part of the foothills of the Himalayas. Many amateur Bigfoot students hotly theorize that these creatures, thought to be long extinct, have managed to survive by retreating ever deeper into the wilderness.

These theorists all tend to start at the beginning place that is itself regarded as controversial by some— the theory of evolution. The theory is widely misunderstood to mean that humans descended from apes, but it actually only holds that somewhere, way back on lines of descent which eventually produced mankind and the various apes, there was a common ancestor with such traits as an opposable thumb and the ability to walk erect. Eventually, from this early species, there evolved both the sophisticated person who drives nervously around on freeways and the primitive apes which munch happily on berries in remote forests.

Profound disagreement comes from people who feel that sacred writings, notably the Bible, must be taken literally. They believe that mankind sprang into being by a single act of divine creation, with no need of ancestors of any kind. In the middle of the spectrum of belief stand people who see no real incompatibility between Bible and science, people who believe that, whether created whole or created through eons by gradual evolution, humanity's history on this planet

41

started with a spark of divine inspiration that gave rise to all life.

For the evolutionists, other candidates for the role of Bigfoot's ancestors include very early and primitive hominids, Java Man and Peking Man, both of which are classified as *Homo erectus*. Fossil evidence found at a famous anthropological site, the caves of Choukoutien in China, indicated Peking Man lived in a cool climate heavily forested with conifers and other trees—very similar to the North American forests where Bigfoot now may walk.

In that scientists now generally agree that the American continent was first populated by humans who walked across a land bridge from Asia in the area now called the Bering Strait, the theory goes that Peking Man, or other living relics of millions of years gone by, could have walked across, too; and it is their great-great-great-great-grandmonsters that are still leaving all those footprints.

No one—not science, not the rank and file of dedicated monster fanciers—really knows if *Gigantopithecus* and *Homo erectus* are really still among us. But huge footprints of mysterious origin are definitely among us, and they have been seen, measured, photographed and cast into molds.

According to an old story, one of the creatures was actually captured. It happened in 1884, as reported by a Canadian newspaper, the *Daily Colonist* of Victoria, British Columbia: The crew of a train, chuffing through a draw in British Columbia, spotted a shaggy half-human, half-ape lying senseless beside the railroad tracks. It had apparently slipped and fallen from the top of the draw. As they approached it, the creature began to regain its senses and tried to get up. It looked smaller than most Sasquatches, just under five-feet tall, according to the train crew. Possibly it was a juvenile, but it looked strange and mean; so one of the engineers walloped it on the head with a rock, stunning it again. Then they tied it up and tossed it in the baggage car and got underway again. The small creature, nick-named "Jacko" by its captors, caused quite a flurry when the train reached its destination. People came from everywhere to see it, marveling at the black silky hair which covered its entire body except for the hands, feet and face. The crowd interest was so intense that an itinerant showman named George Tilbury was prompted to make a fast money offer for Jacko. The train crew, not quite sure what else they could do with their new prisoner, accepted and transferred the crea-ture to Tilbury's care. Science's first known possible chance for a close examination of the Sasquatch vanished over the horizon as Tilbury set off for a "show-business" tour of the old West. No one seems to know what happened to Jacko or Tilbury after that.

But the land was new in those days. As the human population grew and spread out, giant hairy creatures seemingly found themselves confronted by civilization on a more frequent basis. Highways and roads cut through their domains. Tourist hotels and ski resorts popped up to narrow their horizons. Mountain cabins dotted their once empty vistas, followed quickly by housing developments and freeways. In recent years it has become almost common to hear from startled wit-nesses who report seeing dark, shaggy faces staring forlornly over seven-foot fences surrounding their shiny new tract houses.

Shrinkage of wilderness areas may help explain such sudden appearances as that of the Murphysboro Mon-ster, already discussed, or that of Momo, the creature which suddenly surfaced less than 150 miles away, near Louisiana, Missouri, in the summer of 1972.

Momo, who made believers out of a whole passel of cynics from the "show-me" state of Missouri, was first seen by a 15-year-old named Doris Harrison when she looked out of her bathroom window and spotted a tall, hairy creature peering at her house from a hillside. Her father reported what his daughter had seen to the local authorities and that loosed the floodgates. Reports came pouring in from all over town. Someone saw a hairy figure crossing the highway with a dead sheep in its mouth. Another local resident told of seeing a frightening creature with three toes and green eyes. One shaken man called in to say he had just seen a gigantic creature come strolling down the hill next to his house, pause by his driveway long enough to lift his small sports car for a curious look, then drop the car and run away. A couple of youths said the thing had come out of the woods and growled at them. Momo stayed around long enough that summer to give the fledgling journalism students at the nearby University of Missouri something exciting to write about; then, like the nearby Murphysboro visitor, he vanished, it was theorized, into one of the many caves which dot the area.

Of course some experts hold that Momo and the Murphysboro Monster, like the hundreds of other sightings and all those mysterious footprints which keep turning up, are all the work of hoaxers. The former Canadian newspaperman, John Green, a steady, thoughtful Bigfoot investigator who has written numerous articles and two books on the subject, has given a lot of thought to the question.

Green asks, "Is there an unknown species of animal that is very heavy, has humanlike feet and walks erect? The very idea is ridiculous. Is there, then, a person or organization that has been making giant footprints over an area of hundreds of thousands of square miles for the best part of a century? That, too, is ridiculous. The only comfortable explanation is that the tracks don't really exist at all—but the plain fact is that they do."

Dr. John R. Napier, former director of the primate biology program at the Smithsonian Institution, has also

44

written a Bigfoot book and has pondered the question. Upon considering all available evidence, Napier concludes the Abominable Snowman of the Himalayas has little going for it. Except for one photograph of tracks shot at 20,000 feet by Everest mountaineer Eric Shipman, that Napier finds curious and inexplicable, he wryly states he would have no hesitation in "dismissing the Yeti as a red herring, or, at least, as a red bear."

But Bigfoot is a different story. "I am sure that *some* Sasquatch tracks are fakes," Napier says, "but it is beyond reason to suppose that they all are. Indeed, if there was only one real print among 99 fakes it would still be obligatory to explain the real one."

Napier also regards it as difficult to consider every eyewitness account of the many hundreds on record as either a deliberate falsification or a matter of imperfect identification. He concludes:

"The dilemma is simple enough. Either some of the footprints are real, or all are fakes. If they are all fakes, then an explanation invoking legend and folk memory is adequate to explain the mystery. But if any one of them is real, then as scientists we have a lot to explain. Among other things we shall have to rewrite the story of human evolution. We shall have to accept that *Homo sapiens* is not the one and only living product of the hominid line, and we shall have to admit that there are still major mysteries to be solved in a world we thought we knew so well."

Chapter Five

SEARCH FOR THE MISSING LINK

"When you have eliminated the impossible," Sherlock Holmes used to pontificate to Dr. Watson, "whatever

45

remains, however improbable, must be the truth."

The improbable fascinates many monster fanciers. Eager to dream up a method of accounting for the possible existence of such creatures as Bigfoot, one group has even come up with the suggestion that they are "pets" lost from flying saucers during terrestrial landings, or, if you prefer, laboratory animals deliberately left behind by UFO crews to determine whether extraterrestrial creatures can survive here.

But scientific method demands that theories and hypotheses, no matter how intriguing, grow from evidence, and most people are left to try to fit Bigfoot and his cousins into the natural evolutionary lines that eventually gave rise to such other creatures as modern men and apes.

Regrettably, however, if you want to examine the skulls and skeletons of such a prime candidate as Peking Man for a linkage to Bigfoot, you run smack into a real-life mystery that would rival espionage fiction and wild adventure novels for strange twists and turns.

Because Peking Man, a possible "missing link," is himself missing.

Discovered in 1926, the fossil remains of this prehistoric man mysteriously disappeared in the turmoil that followed Pearl Harbor on December 7, 1941. The priceless bits of bone are still the object of an all-out, modern-day search.

It is necessary to go back to one of the more recent developments in the search for Peking Man. . . .

It is July 27, 1972. Christopher G. Janus, a wealthy, 62-year-old Chicago stockbroker, is on a high-speed elevator, whooshing upwards in the Empire State Building, more than a quarter-mile above the heart of muggy Manhattan. Janus is keyed up, a little tense, but it isn't the fear of heights that people so often feel at the top of the Empire State Building.

Will she be there? She swore she would come, but

46

Janus can't be sure. When she telephoned, Janus had suggested that she meet him for lunch, but the whispery voice on the other end of the line had said no, no, she was afraid to be seen with him. He had been forced to talk hard and persuasively even to get her to agree to meet him anonymously at the Empire State observatory.

Tourists are everywhere when he gets off the elevator. The gray-haired Janus, strongly built for a man in his sixties, tries conscientiously to look just like another sightseer. The vast sweep of the city—its coiling rivers, its broad avenues—unwinds before his eyes from the observation deck. There to the northwest, that's the United Nations tower. Spotting it is appropriate. His mission, in a curious way, is so similar to that of the UN: improving the relations between nations. If only—

"Mr. Janus?" the voice says uncertainly at his elbow. He turns. She's nervous, that's for sure. Even his slight movement makes her jump. He smiles at her reassuringly, showing white teeth. His eyes rapidly assess the middle-aged woman standing beside him. The widow of a Marine who died seven years ago, she told Janus on the phone. And the electrifying words, *"He left me a wooden chest. It contains the bones. It is my legacy."*

Janus now speaks to the woman, doing his best to calm her down, to give her confidence. He has to have evidence, he explains. He has to have proof. Finally she nods and draws a photograph from her purse.

There, in a picture of some kind of a sturdy box, is the dome of a skull. Fragments of other bones that could be parts of a skull, others that might be a shoulder blade, parts of leg bones, all lie in a grisly jumble. A fever flares in Janus's blood as he stares at the photograph. The bones look human.

"Where are the bones now?" he asks excitedly. "When can I examine them?"

"I must be extremely careful," the woman says. She

47

takes the picture back. "My husband warned me to be extremely careful with the bones."

"Of course," Janus says, "but——"

"He told me they were priceless," the woman says stiffly. "But they were ill-gotten. They were smuggled out of China at great personal risk."

Another group of sightseers pours from the direction of the elevators, squealing and laughing. Janus and the woman move a few feet closer to the edge of the observation deck where they can be alone.

Janus says, "As to the legal liability, we can't know——"

But suddenly the woman whirls, and her face goes white.

"What is it?" Janus says. He looks around quickly, but he sees only the tourists surging toward them, jostling for positions at the rail. Then he sees a man in a light green-plaid jacket, pointing a Kodak Signet 35 vaguely in their direction, trying to focus in on the sprawling cityscape.

"It's a trap," the woman gasps. She glares at Janus for half a heartbeat, then rams the photograph back in her purse and runs for the elevator, shielding her face from the bewildered amateur photographer as she hurries past him.

More tourists flood from the constantly shuttling elevators. The woman ducks through them, but Janus is cut off. He tries to make his way around them, but it is too late. She's already into an elevator. The door is closing. Janus's heart sinks with the elevator. She's gone. And he doesn't know her name, nor her address, nor even what town she lives in. New York? That would mean he has only 8,000,000 people to sift through.

Such a little quirk of fate, a man choosing that split-second to raise a camera. And in that one split-second, chance has snatched out of his hands the opportunity

48

to solve one of science's greatest mysteries: Where is Peking Man?

New facts have now been added to the baffling case of the Peking Man, the invaluable relic whose 500,000-year-old remains were first unearthed near Peking a half-century ago, only to disappear 15 years later.

Accusations, bitter feelings, international politics, rumors, violence, conflicting stories—all have dogged the ghostly footsteps of this prehistoric being whose remains are beyond price to frustrated scientists and are revered as a national treasure by the People's Republic of China.

"Help us find the Peking Man," Janus was implored in China in June,1972 when, in the wake of President Nixon's peace mission to China, Janus visited there on behalf of a foundation sponsoring teacher-student exchanges and cultural symposiums. "Anyone who brings back the Peking Man," he was told, "will be a hero to the Chinese people."

Janus immediately threw himself into the search upon his return and offered a $5,000 reward for information leading to the recovery of the relics. He was soon on the track of two hot leads. Several hundred replies poured in from people who read newspaper stories about the search, and one had a ring of authenticity. A Chinese-born New York businessman contacted him with the information that a "friend in Taiwan" who was high in the Chiang Kai-shek regime had a footlocker filled with Peking Man fossils.

Janus met with the businessman and was told that a great deal of violence had been connected with getting the fossils, and that the Taiwanese family was terribly afraid. But if there was enough money involved, the businessman thought the family might be willing to hand over the fossils. The money eventually mentioned was in the neighborhood of $750,000. Janus said he

49

wanted to see evidence first, and negotiations began slowly.

In the meantime, while he was still in New York talking over arrangements, Janus received the anonymous telephone call from the mysterious widow who then met him on top of the Empire State Building, only to flee without telling him her name or where she could be contacted.

What could he do? He waited, trying to control his impatience, one day optimistic that she would call again, discouraged the next. Finally, on a long shot, he placed a classified ad that ran at the bottom of page one in *The New York Times*. It said:

PEKING MAN. Emp St? Obs. mtg. Funds
avail; no questions. Phone C.G.J.

He had little hope. A week passed, Then, out of the blue, there was the voice again on the other end of the telephone.

"I have to be extremely careful," the voice whispered. "The fossils are stolen property."

"But you didn't steal them," Janus pointed out. "You're only in possession of them. Maybe you're not even legally liable. We can find out. But the first step is, you must send me a copy of the picture so I can have the fossils authenticated."

"How do I know that someone will not authenticate them away from me?" she said reluctantly. "I tell you, they're stolen property."

Over and over, she nervously referred to the priceless fossils by that term, "stolen property," and Janus heard nothing further from the cautious widow. But he got one big break: A copy of the photograph did arrive in the mail, and he took it promptly to a leading authority on the search for Peking Man, Dr. Harry L. Shapiro, curator emeritus of physical anthropology at the American Museum of Natural History.

For more than a year, the eminent scientist had been following new leads of his own in the frustrating case of Peking Man. Now, from a totally unexpected source, in a poor-quality photograph of a wooden chest of bones, he saw a thrilling sight: "The skull has the shape of the Peking Man," Shapiro concluded. "A photograph can be misleading. But it's promising."

More Shapiro would not say, not until he could inspect the fossils themselves, but a wave of fresh hope swept the worldwide scientific community. After despairing for three decades that the world-famous collection had been irretrievably lost, there was now at least a possibility that Peking Man would be rediscovered.

Peking Man is actually the remains of some 40 early beings who lived and died in what scientists regard as the morning of mankind. This is one reason the collection is so extraordinarily important. Most traces of primitive man are pitifully few—a single tooth here, there a jawbone, elsewhere a fragment of a skull. Peking Man is the world's richest collection of bones and artifacts for a single group of primitive man found to date, the first known community of early people, and therefore incredibly valuable.

What can you discover from such a collection? In the case of Peking Man, simple stone tools were unearthed; these "men" had invented tools. There was a layer of ashes; they had already found fire. Animal bones whispered that these creatures were hunters who brought their prey back to their caves. Hackberry seeds found between the teeth of some specimens said that they ate fruits. The way some skulls were crushed from the side, toothmarks on discarded bones, told a gory tale of violence and cannibalism.

New scientific techniques have been developed over the last 30 years that can lead to far more sophisticated information. But with the disappearance of the bones in World War Two, Peking Man's story was snapped off like a broken film. Although casts were made, they are not adequate for the kind of detailed study possible today.

The mysterious saga of Peking Man started in the great cave of Choukoutien, near Peking. Years of sleuthing went into the mere finding of the cave.

The first clue? "Dragon's bones," found in an apothecary shop in Peking in 1901. As all Chinese knew, the fossils of "dragons" dug up in the fields by Chinese peasants were strong medicine. Ground up, tossed into a cup of tea, they cured everything from measles to senility. But a German engineer named K. A. Haberer had a different idea. He prowled the Chinese drugstores and bought up a big collection of "dragon's teeth" that turned out to be the fossilized remains not only of orangutans, pandas, tigers and deer, but also of mammals that had become extinct. The most remarkable tooth was extremely worn, extremely old and extremely human.

Somewhere in the Peking area was an answer to the mystery of man's ancient past, and an international group of scientists began tracking the dragon bones back to their lair. One was a young Swedish geologist, Gunnar Andersson. It was 1918, and he trudged the barren hills 40 miles to the southwest of Peking, prospecting for minerals in limestone bedrock that here and there had accumulated pockets of red sun-baked clay. But mineral deposits weren't his only interest, and he discovered a vast deposit of perfectly preserved mammal fossils.

The deposit was too rich for one man to explore

adequately. In 1920, Andersson returned with two colleagues, including an American Museum of Natural History paleontologist, and the first tentative excavations began.

Then, in 1926, the first big news exploded on the world. In a blaze of publicity it was announced that two fossil teeth dug up were unmistakably human. Peking Man, buried for a half-million years, began to emerge from the cave that was to become world famous —the cave of Choukoutien.

By then, turmoil was already ripping China apart. Antagonism toward foreigners ran high. Warlords locked together in death struggles, disrupting the countryside. The digging at Choukoutien went on, and scientists locked together in their own bitter struggles. Was *Sinanthropus pekinensis,* as the fossils were first classified, a man or an ape? Had a whole new genus been found, or was this "Peking Man" only one of a genus of previously discovered early humans?

During 15 years of digging, rich finds of skulls and numerous other bones settled the scientific dispute, but the other battle got hotter and hotter. To civil war was added the new threat of invasion of China by the Japanese. The stage was being set for the disappearance of this new variety of humankind, Peking Man.

First, the "father" of Peking Man, Canadian anatomist Dr. Davidson Black, was killed by his "offspring." Working doggedly in his laboratory in Peking, he laboriously cleaned each new find that came to light. Dr. Black coughed a little in the clouds of fine dust kicked up by the sensitive dental drill he used to clean centuries of dirt off the bones. Soon he was coughing more. In 1934, he died—his lungs ruined by the dust he had inhaled.

His successor in charge of studying the fossils, Dr. Franz Weidenreich, soon had an equally anguishing problem. To his fellow scientists at the lab—the Cenozoic Research Laboratory at Peking Union Medical College—it may have seemed one winter day as if the German's frown was directed at a slender, splintered fragment of bone he was examining. He put it gently back in a tray filled with a pile of dusty bones and picked up a femur from another tray.

Dr. W. H. Wong and Dr. T. H. Yin studied Weidenreich's frown. They exchanged looks, but they were too polite to comment directly. Weidenreich answered their unspoken question by asking another.

His strong German accent almost obscuring the words, he said, "My friends, today and tomorrow and for who knows how long we have a great problem. My friends, how can we insure the safety of these fragile bones?"

Because a holocaust was coming. It would be known as World War Two.

The remains of Peking Man escaped the first flood of Japanese forces into northern China in 1937 because they were kept in the American-owned college, and Japan and the United States were still on friendly terms. But Weidenreich knew that more trouble was on its way. He had seen that kind of trouble before—in 1934, when he left Germany because his Jewish origins made it no longer safe to stay. The United States, it became terrifyingly apparent, was being drawn into the conflict.

For the last crucial months in 1941, Dr. Weidenreich and his colleagues watched the gathering storm. In memos, letters and conferences in the dusty lab, they considered the options open to them. The fossils could be hidden in a secret vault in Peking. Or they could be sent to southwest China, where there was less turmoil. Or they could be sent out of the country, to the United States.

The trouble was, they had to be sent secretly. They

were, literally, invaluable, and the risk of trying to transport them through a war-torn countryside was great. Weidenreich spent sleepless nights and anxious days.

Then the inevitable happened. The storm clouds of war now gathered directly overhead, and Dr. Weidenreich was ordered back to the States. He made a last desperate attempt to convince the U. S. ambassador in Peking to send the fossils out in official baggage so they would not be discovered, but it was a sad and apprehensive scientist who reported back to Drs. Wong and Yin.

"My friends," Weidenreich said heavily, "I have failed."

Wong and Yin had tried to prepare themselves for this. "What shall we do?" Dr. Wong asked quietly.

"The decision must be made now," Dr. Yin agreed.

"It is too great a risk to try to smuggle out the originals as part of my baggage," the worried Weidenreich told them. "If the fossils were discovered by the customs control at an embarkation or transit point, they could be confiscated."

Dr. Yin nodded, adding reluctantly, "In addition, it must be taken into account that the objects are too valuable to expose them to an unprotected voyage in so dangerous a time."

Dr. Weidenreich sighed. "Considering all the pros and cons, we have no choice. It would be wisest to leave the originals where they are now—that is, in the safe in the Cenozoic Research Laboratory at P.U.M.C."

So Dr. Weidenreich had to leave China, taking with him only photographs, detailed drawings and casts carefully prepared so he could complete his study of Peking Man.

On December 7, 1941, came Pearl Harbor and despair. Dr. Weidenreich, now safe in America, could only worry and wonder: What would become of the precious bones?

He had reason to worry. As the Japanese moved to seize the American Embassy in Peking, the Chinese government, in a panicky decision, turned over the bones to the United States Marines leaving the city in the final days before war broke out. Mrs. Claire Taschidjian, who settled down after the war in New York City's borough of Queens, worked at the Peking laboratory. She remembered that she packed the bones in two redwood chests, but other stories eventually made the rounds. News reports of the time say they were wrapped in officers' clothing. And a distinguished New York heart specialist, Dr. William T. Foley, has revealed that he saw some of the fossils packed in large glass jars and placed in military footlockers, but he left the city before the shipment was complete and ready to go.

All that is known for sure is that Peking Man departed Peking for elsewhere. Then he disappeared. And he disappeared as he had appeared—piecemeal. Following the best information available, here is what happened.

The 220-man detachment of China Marines of the Old Corps stationed in Peking had handled some strange assignments before, but this was certainly one of the weirdest. It was a few days before Pearl Harbor, and they'd be leaving any minute, heading for the S. S. President Harrison and, hopefully, home. Now their commander, Colonel William W. Ashurst, came up with this crazy business—chaperoning a collection of old bones, when they were none too sure they could get out of China themselves!

The boxes of bones were heavy, but the North China Marines, as they called themselves, shouldered them willingly once they knew what all the fuss was about.

"They're prehistoric," confided Gerald L. Beeman of Bellbrook, Ohio, one of the Marine embassy guards.

"Sure, they're a million years old," laughed the detachment wag, young Frank Whitehead, a native of Nashville, Tennessee.

Actually, of course, it is thought the bones were only a half-million years old, but Whitehead could give or take a few hundred thousand as easily as he could roll a few rounds of poker dice at one of Peking's darkened bars. The bones were loaded to his cheerful yodeling, "Dem bones, dem bones, dem dry bones," and for once his companions didn't yell the customary, "Pipe down, Whitehead." They were a group of worried men, the North China Marines, preparing to be evacuated from China on Tuesday, 9 December 1941, and they were anxious to get going. A little joking didn't hurt their spirits any as they thought of all their guns, ammunition and other equipment that they'd already hastily loaded for shipment. Destination: the little Marine outpost of Camp Holcomb in the coastal town of Chinwangtao.

There were at least two consignments of fossils, one labeled with the name of Colonel Ashurst, and one with the name of a young Marine medical officer, Dr. William T. Foley, who had just completed a three-year term of duty in China and was en route home. The colonel ordered Dr. Foley to carry part of the endangered fossils along with him in his personal baggage.

Whitehead was still singing and cracking bad minstrel jokes to a box he called "Mr. Bones" when the Marines' gear was shipped out on the Manchurian railway.

Some say a hospital corpsman was designated to accompany the bones but missed the train. Some say the Japanese looted the baggage train before it reached Camp Holcomb, taking not only blankets and other Marine equipment that was later found in a concentration camp near the area, but also the bones of Peking Man.

Again, maybe. But Herman Davis, later Dr. Foley's assistant in New York and then a young pharmacist's mate stationed with Dr. Foley's unit at Camp Holcomb, remembered vividly being asked by Dr. Foley to receive a batch of footlockers sent in his name there and take care of them as personal baggage.

Davis unloaded Foley's baggage from the train. He had no idea some of Foley's footlockers contained fossils. He didn't open them, just piled them in his room at the camp.

Then, on December 8, the day after Pearl Harbor, the small Marine outpost was surrounded by Japanese soldiers. In the harbor, a Japanese cruiser appeared. Overhead six Japanese planes were sighted.

"You must surrender," a Japanese spokesman informed Davis and his companions. But Marines don't surrender easily; North China Marines less easily still. They refused, and sent the spokesman packing.

"I'm gonna radio our headquarters in Peking," the C.O. of the outpost told his men.

"What do we do in the meantime?" a young Marine drawled, trying to look as tough as his buddies.

"What do you think?" the C.O snapped. "We fight."

Davis was ready, and he got readier fast. He hauled the Foley footlockers over to a window to use as a barricade, and slapped his machine gun on top of them, ready for anything, without realizing that he was using one of the world's most precious scientific collections as a makeshift fortress.

But Peking Man was not to end his 500,000-year career in a blazing fire-fight on that December day. At the last moment the Marines were ordered by their headquarters to surrender without a suicidal battle, and Davis was shipped off to imprisonment in a nearby city,

Tientsin. The baggage was left behind, and the Japanese swooped in, looting as they went.

It took 30 years for this to become known, but Peking Man did not vanish at that point. In April, 1971 Dr. Foley, no longer a very junior officer who relied on senior officers to conduct the search for Peking Man, but a respected Manhattan physician writing his memoirs, realized that he might have exclusive information on the missing fossils. He contacted Dr. Shapiro of the Natural History Museum, and together they related a dramatic tale.

Think how you would have felt if you had been young Bill Foley in 1941. Don't you suppose you might have clenched your fist at an unkind fate? Your tour of duty just completed, on December 9 you would have been on that ship. First Manila, then home, and nothing could look sweeter than those grimy sidewalks of good old New York. New York, too, was where you could shed the staggering responsibility of the Peking Man fossils that your commander, Colonel Ashurst, asked you to deliver safely to the States.

Instead, on December 7, you were arrested. Oh, there was no rough stuff. You were a young medical officer, and Japanese tradition required that courtesy and respect be shown even for junior rank. After about a week they even allowed you to go back to your house in Tientsin. They gave you semi-diplomatic status. You were allowed the freedom of the city.

When your country is at war, you don't really care much about politeness. But soon, you're forced to care. You can't believe your eyes. Footlockers painted with your name come tagging along to you in Tientsin. Stiffly proper where officers are concerned, the Japanese hadn't even ransacked the footlockers, and nothing is missing from your personal belongings except

several modern skulls you kept as anatomical specimens.

But what really makes your eyes pop open is the
realization that you are in possession of the world's
hottest potatoes. Among your baggage you recognize
footlockers assigned to you by your colonel in Peking,
containing the priceless Peking Man fossils!

What are you going to do? You face internment—
four years of it, the way things turn out. What can you
possibly do to safeguard those ancient bones? Where
can you hide them, when the Japanese could come beat-
ing on your door at any moment?

Young Bill Foley never looked in the Peking Man
footlockers. As fast as he could, he sent some of the
boxes to the Swiss Warehouse in Tientsin, others to the
Pasteur Institute there, still others to the homes of three
Chinese friends he felt he could rely on.

Then he was picked up. Declared a prisoner of war,
Foley was shipped to a prison camp near Shanghai with
the rest of the Marine detachment. *He never saw those
Peking Man footlockers again.*

One last footlocker, one precious footlocker, is the
last piece in the puzzle, and for nearly four years the
North China Marines succeeded in hiding it in three
different concentration camps. This footlocker carried
the name of Colonel Ashurst, the detachment's commander, and for reasons known only to him he considered it to contain the most precious of all the fossils.

By now, the Japanese had been tipped off by a Tokyo
anthropologist about the famous fossils, and Foley's lug-
gage was searched repeatedly, but the Marine POW's
managed to hide *THE* box through the years, and
through the moves, usually by burying it under their
quarters. At the Chung Wan camp, at the Fungtai
camp—the Marines stubbornly continued their sleight

60

of hand with "Mr. Bones." The last Dr. Foley saw of the box was in 1945, when he and Colonel Ashurst parted company, "I to an iron mine in northern Japan and the latter to Hokkaido," Foley later remembered.

And the last box, after surviving so many hazards, disappeared. Colonel Ashurst died a few years after the war, and if he ever confided in anyone what happened to the precious box, the secret has remained well-guarded.

Where are the bones now? What about the "friend in Taiwan" and the Empire State woman? Were they really con artists, trying to make a quick buck from a concerned community of scientists and philanthropists? No, the two leads picked up by the stockbroker-turned-detective, Christopher G. Janus, could both be authentic. We believe that at least a portion of Dr. Foley's warehoused footlockers may well have been spirited out of China after the war when the Nationalists were forced to retreat from the mainland, and are now in the nervous hands of the "friend in Taiwan." The buried footlocker from the POW camp could have been dug up after the Japanese surrender by one of the last remaining captive Marines, and ended up years later as the legacy of the Marine widow who appeared at the top of the Empire State Building.

So at least as late as 1972, while Janus was still receiving "funny" telephone calls at home from anonymous voices which told him to "lay off or you'll be sorry," there was somewhere in the U. S. a frightened woman who may have a share of the world's most sought after collection of prehistoric bones. And somewhere in Taiwan was a jumpy official who feels, Janus has been told, that the search for the bones is endangering his life.

Then why would they still be holding the bones? Why hide such a collection of hot potatoes when they bring

61

only danger and despair? Mainly because they're afraid of what would happen if they admitted having them. The bones are too valuable to ditch, too hot to display, too well-known to sell. That leaves only confession and possible prosecution for theft of a national treasure.

Even if one or both of the Janus leads were to prove out and the bones are ransomed back into the scientific world, the mystifying saga of Peking Man will not end.

There were too many fossils, too many consignments spread out over too many hiding places. It will be a long time before "dem bones" all get connected back again. Some may still be gathering dust in mainland China, waiting for the men, long since dead, who hid them. Some may have drifted to this country in the souvenir kits of returning servicemen.

So if you had an uncle or a father or a grandfather who served in the Pacific theater during World War Two, you may well have bits and pieces of Peking Man at the bottom of a trunk in your own attic.

How about it? Do you know where the rest of Peking Man is?

Study of the fossils with the sophisticated techniques now available to science could be a beginning place to solve many riddles. For instance, if Peking Man is an ancestor not only of modern man, but of a manlike creature variously called Bigfoot, Sasquatch or the Abominable Snowman, great changes would necessarily have taken place in the last 500,000 years.

Since science thinks Peking Man knew the use of tools and fire and, it is inferred, hunted big game, something dire has happened since to his possible Bigfoot offspring. While there are eyewitness reports of Bigfoot creatures creeping close to a hunter's fire or, as in the case of the Russian Alma, warming themselves at abandoned fires, there is no record of their using fire for themselves, much less of their making or using tools. And the scanty record on their eating habits runs mostly to a vegetarian's diet, with a few mice as a change of pace.

If science could learn more about Peking Man, maybe it could learn more about what might have happened to produce a Bigfoot. Or maybe not. Research is like that. But until and unless the Peking Man fossils show up, that avenue of research will be forever closed.

Chapter Six

MONSTERS OF THE DEEP

Even if Peking Man helps solve the mystery of manlike monsters, there will still be unanswered questions about a wide variety of other possible prehistoric predators.

For example, in the historic highlands of Scotland lies a long, narrow slash of deep water. A sea loch with raised beaches standing 50 feet above sea level, this body of water rests at the edge of Invermoristan Forest. Bleached white shells litter the raised beaches, relics of prehistory when it was once an arm of the Atlantic Ocean, back before the Ice Age covered Scotland with a two-mile-deep carpet of ice. When the ice melted, the runoff filled the loch and the land surrounding it rose, cutting it off from the ocean, creating one of the most unique lakes in the world.

The great, land-locked loch is like practically no other body of water known to man. Twenty-four miles long by one mile wide, it has no islands. Its walls slope straight down. Its bottom, unnaturally flat, is 700 feet deep, deeper even than the average depth of the North Sea. It holds an extraordinary amount of water. It also holds clues to one of the most intriguing so-called underwater monsters in modern history, the world's most publicized and controversial sea creature—the Loch Ness Monster, known affectionately to millions since 1933 as "Nessie."

Loch Ness was once filled with saltwater, back when it was a part of the sea, but time and nature changed all that when rivers dumped miles and miles of silt into the loch over the hundreds of years that followed the Ice Age and blocked the seaward end, making it a self-contained lake. The original seawater was gradually changed to freshwater, but the change took place so slowly that marine creatures which had been trapped by the silt dam had many generations to adapt themselves.

"Nessie," if she exists, is probably a descendant of one of these sea creatures, gradually evolving from an ocean-going inhabitant to a more dormant land-locked freshwater denizen of the lake. She may have been around for a long time. Isolated reports have cropped up for hundreds of years from Scots who passed through the area about "some turr-ible monster" thrashing in the lake.

Then in 1933, something new happened, and the world sat up and began to pay closer attention to Nessie. Until that year, the only route to the loch was an old road along the southern shore, built after the Jacobite Rising in 1715 in order to open up the isolated, rebellious highlands. The road ran mainly through the hills, and even when it touched the shore it didn't offer much of a view, thanks to a heavy growth of trees and brush.

But in the early thirties, work began on a new road along the north shore. The shrubbery was cleared away and the dynamite blasting began, to clear away the rocks and make room for the road crews. Some say the noise of the blasting woke up Nessie and brought her to the surface to see what was happening.

There may have been a number of sightings in those early days of the thirties, but the first to be widely reported by the news media took place from the new road on April 14, 1933. The witnesses were a hotel owner named John Mackay and his wife, who lived near Inverness.

Mr. and Mrs. Mackay, chugging along in their old auto, were headed down the road when there was a sudden disturbance of the water out in the lake. Mrs. Mackay saw it first. She touched her husband's arm and said, "John, look. There's something in the lake. What is it?"

Mackay couldn't really hear her, not over the noisy racket of the auto engine, but he glanced in the direction of her pointing arm and saw the roiling water for himself. He quickly yanked his hand brake, squealing the little car to a halt, and watched, wondering what it could be. What he and his wife saw stunned them both almost beyond words.

There, out in the lake, rising above the flat, calm surface, water cascading from its back and churning into a lake so dark with tints of peat that it looked like acres of black glass, was Nessie—an unknown creature which looked at first like only an enormous black hump in a patch of foam. What on earth was it? Some kind of practical joke? Had the road crews left something behind, something which floated out there to surprise and baffle the early users of the road?

But no. As they sat in the car and watched, the creature continued to rise until the Mackays could see that it appeared to be some kind of prehistoric reptile over 60 feet long. Body like a whale. Long neck. Small head.

"Oh, John, what *is* it?" Mrs. Mackay asked again.

Her husband shook his head, too shaken to speak. She urged him to drive on, but he could only sit there and stare at it writhing out in the water. It stayed on the surface for almost a full minute before it seemed to become aware of their presence. Then it quickly dived out of sight.

The Mackays didn't know quite what to do. They felt they ought to tell someone, but they were afraid people might think they were crazy. Besides, if word got out about there being monsters in the lake, wasn't that likely to scare potential customers away from their hotel? No one likes to vacation in a place where he might get eaten up by a monster. (There were skeptics in those days, including the *New York Herald Tribune,* which covered the story and claimed that the Mackays knew perfectly well that stories of a mysterious monster would attract customers, not repel them.)

The Mackays finally decided to tell their story to a Scottish newsman named Alex Campbell, but only if he promised not to use their names. And the first modern "Nessie story" appeared in print on May 2 in the *Inverness Courier.* Within a week, the story of the sighting of a creature had been picked up by a rival paper, the *Northern Chronicle,* and the creature was dubbed "The Loch Ness Monster" in its headline. The name has been with us ever since.

Even so, Nessie might have been a flash in the pan, quickly reported and just as quickly forgotten by newspapers, had it not been for continued sightings. Additional visual contacts through the summer were duly reported by the world's press, eager for a lively story that would keep their readers entertained. No one took the stories seriously as yet, except for a few organizations which felt they could profit from the monster. An English circus offered 20,000 pounds for the animal if it could be delivered alive. The New York Zoo came up with an offer of $5,000. Local lake inhabitants started to worry and complained about outsiders after their "very own monster," until the chief constable of Inverness finally issued an order banning attempts to capture or molest the monster.

But the real excitement started later that year when someone took the first photograph of Nessie.

It was Sunday, November 12, 1933, seven months after the first sighting. By now there had been 51 reported eyewitnesses. The story still rippled through the world's front pages from time to time, but people were no longer so easily entertained by it. After all, sightings could be explained as tricks of the eyesight, lies on the part of publicity seekers, the fevered imagination of a few nuts, anything.

But on that Sunday in November, a man named Hugh Gray was wandering near his house on the lake shore at Foyers. The weather was cold, and there was snow lying in the steep slopes above the lake. The wind, out of the north, was whipping up whitecaps. Gray, a photography enthusiast, was carrying his camera, looking for nature subjects, and, as he has admitted, halfway hoping to catch a glimpse of this so-called monster reported by so many of his friends and neighbors.

He had just climbed a rocky cliff that rose about 30 feet above the surface of the lake. The view was good. The cliff overlooked the water from a distance of about half a mile. Suddenly, the water began to churn. A large shape loomed out of the water, thrashing through the whitecaps. Gray shivered with excitement and began to shoot pictures as fast as he could. The creature looked as if it had a long body with a slender neck, but he couldn't see it too clearly because of all the spray it was throwing off. He managed to get five pictures before it dived out of sight.

"I saw an unco' sight," Gray told his brother breathlessly when he got home. "The beast in the loch!" A very large body, he said, dark grayish in color, with skin that appeared to be smooth and shiny.

"Och, awa'!" his brother scoffed. Gray insisted he had seen it, and further that he had photographs to prove it.

Since Gray was an ordinary citizen rather than a newspaperman, it apparently never occurred to him that time might be important to a news story. He put his camera away in a drawer and left it there. Three weeks passed before the brother, eager to see if such pictures were actually on the film, took the camera out of the drawer and carried the film off to Inverness to have it developed. Four of the five pictures came out blank. But the fifth showed an odd wormlike shape, surrounded by mist and spray, weaving through the water.

The photograph was published on December 6 by the Scottish *Daily Record*. Instantly the story of Nessie took on new dimensions. Newspapers everywhere reproduced the picture. Technicians at Eastman Kodak were asked to examine the negative to see if it had been tampered with (they certified that it had not). Zoologists were asked to look at the picture and offer their expert opinions. Scientists offered a variety of explanations—that it might be a bottle-nosed whale, one of the larger species of shark, or that it might even be a rotting tree trunk, forced to the surface by its own decomposing gases. In general, scientists were unimpressed, but the public fancy was captured.

Other photographs followed. The most famous is probably one taken in April, 1934 by a London doctor, Kenneth Wilson. Dr. Wilson, returning from a vacation in northern Scotland to his London home, was passing through the Loch Ness area when he stopped for a short rest near Ivermoriston, on the road to Inverness. As he stood beside his car, his eyes were drawn to a commotion out on the lake. Something broke through the surface of the water and raised up. The head of some strange animal.

Wilson was carrying a friend's camera in his car. He had borrowed it to take pictures of trains in northern Scotland. He quickly leaned through his car window and grabbed the camera. Hurrying down the slope toward the water, he focused his lens on the apparition. He managed to shoot four plates of the creature before it vanished.

As soon as the doctor reached Inverness, he took the plates to a chemist named Morrison and had them developed. As with Gray, two of the plates turned out blank. But the other two held images. One showed a long neck arching high above the water, and the other showed the head dropping down, about to disappear. The better of the two pictures, the one of the long arching neck, was sold to the *Daily Mail*. The other might have disappeared over the years, except that Morrison, the chemist, kept a copy of it.

Dr. Wilson's picture has been reproduced many times. It is probably the clearest of the many pictures that others have captured over the years. But to be completely objective, we have to state that the photograph would be easier to accept as that of some large, mysterious creature were it not for the ripples surrounding the beast. To the practiced eye, these ripples simply appear to be too small in scope, as though the pictured monster might be only a foot or two in height. Many people disagree, but the possibility of a hoax does exist.

Nor are hoaxes unknown when it comes to tracking Nessie. In December, 1933, just as the stories of the Loch Ness creature were beginning to receive serious attention, a man named Weatheral (he told local lake inhabitants he was a big-game hunter) and a friend came to the lake, sponsored by the *Daily Mail,* to search for the creature. The two men rented a boat and scoured the lake for several days. On December 20, the self-styled white hunter and his companion "chanced" across a track made by the monster—a giant footprint along the shore.

Local people were dubious at first, since they had been looking unsuccessfully for just such footprints themselves. But the men produced a plaster cast they had made of the footprint. It was about eight inches across, with undulating pads and the outlines of claws or nails. Weatheral, a self-proclaimed expert, announced that the beast was a very powerful, four-footed animal about 20 feet long with soft pads.

Unfortunately for Weatheral, a cast of the footprint was delivered to the British Museum for examination. A few days later, two museum experts announced they could find little difference between the footprint of the Loch Ness Monster and the footprint of a hippopotamus. In fact, the footprint was queerly like that which would be made by a mounted hippo foot turned into an umbrella stand by dealers in African curios, if an umbrella stand chanced to go for a walk by an isolated loch.

The *Daily Mail,* embarrassed by its part in the footprint adventure, backed away, red-faced.

At about the same time the "footprint" was being discovered, another luckless eyewitness claimed he really did see the monster ashore.

Arthur Grant, a young medical student, was on his way home by motorcycle on the night of January 5, 1934. It was past midnight, and the sky was dark and starless, thanks to a heavy overcast. About three miles from Lochend, the clouds suddenly broke and a bright moon drenched the roadside.

Grant thought he saw something ahead, a massive dark object among the bushes side of the road to his right. As his motorcycle putted noisily along the road, something huge bounded out of the bushes, undulated across the road in two great strides and vanished into the undergrowth.

Startled nearly out of his wits, Grant skidded to a halt and, more foolhardy than brave, raced after the creature. But it rushed for the shore and dived in with a great splash. Grant marked the spot so he could find it later and hurried on home to wake his younger brothers and tell them, "I've seen it!" He even made a sketch of it to show them how it looked.

By the time Grant went back to the scene the next day, word had spread about his midnight encounter. Weatheral, the gamehunter, showed up, and the two of them were photographed together inspecting the area for footprints. Down on the beach someone found the carcass of a goat, and much was made of the monster's obvious meat-eating tendencies. Another footprint was located, too, but the memory of the hippopotamus foot had spoiled interest in tracks and no one gave it much thought.

Sightings continued, but became less frequent. People began to suspect it all was a publicity hoax to try and lure tourists into the area. Nessie was allowed to sink of her own weight for almost 26 years. Sure, there were continuing reports, but if there was something out there, it had apparently gotten over the noise of the blasting and the road-building in the thirties, and it seemed content to spend most of its time under the water, surfacing only often enough to keep the story going in an occasional Sunday newspaper supplement.

Then, in 1960, the story was suddenly alive and kicking again.

This time a film strip shot by a man named Tim Dinsdale revived it. Dinsdale, intrigued by the continuing reports and a book that had been published about the deep-lake monster, borrowed a 16 mm movie camera and went to Loch Ness determined to get pictures of the creature if it existed. He spent several months on the lake, looking for the best possible position. Finally, in April, 1960, he managed to get a few feet of film of something moving across the lake near Foyers. It was some kind of a hump, reddish brown in color, and it moved first to the right, then the left, then parallel to the opposite shore.

Dinsdale's film was shown on British television, creating an instant sensation. Scientists weren't convinced yet, but other Nessie fans began to flock once more to the lake for a look. Nessie became almost as important a money-making item for the area as Scotch whiskey.

Then came a turning point in the history of the lake monster. A Royal Air Force photo-intelligence outfit known as the Joint Air Reconnaissance Intelligence Center (JARIC) examined Dinsdale's film. They analyzed it carefully, through optical enlargements of each frame, and announced that it was neither a boat nor any other mechanical contrivance, but rather appeared to be an animate object some six feet wide, of indeterminate length, traveling through the water at about 10 miles per hour.

Their report, some 2,000 words long and couched in guarded military terminology, left only one possible conclusion: that Loch Ness holds some massive object in its depths, probably alive.

Since Jaric was a highly respected RAF unit, the same outfit that had analyzed long-range aerial photographs and detected Germany's secret buzz-bomb bases during World War Two, everyone suddenly took notice. Could there really be a Nessie? Was it not a hoax after all?

Scientists began to flock to the lake for a closer look.

The first serious scientific activity took place in 1962, when an organization named The Loch Ness Phenomena Investigation Bureau Ltd. set up headquarters and began to analyze all monster sightings. The LNPIB, as it is called for short, is made up of volunteer members and has been on the lake ever since. It keeps cameras permanently mounted, assists other investigation teams, files and catalogues reports.

At first, the new expeditions tried underwater microphones, night sweeps of the lake (on the theory that the

Tracks, screams
Big muddy 'critter' sighted at Big Muddy

TUE JUN 26 1973

Is there really a monster from the Big Muddy River?

Murphysboro police and Jackson County authorities spent several hours early today trying to find out.

The answer is still awaited:

The physical facts included:

A couple parked near the boat launch area just east of Riverside Park said they definitely saw something about midnight;

Police found tracks near the scene;

Police heard unusual screams in the distance, while checking the scene.

Murphysboro Police sai...

had seen what he described as a "7-foot-tall mud-covered and light-haired man" walking toward his car.

A companion in the car reported she had heard screams, shortly before the man was seen.

The man told police he saw the man walking toward his car, and "took off."

Police returned to the scene and found footprints area where the he had see...

Poli...

Southern Illinoisan reports first sighting of the Murphysboro Monster.

Conqueror of Everest Sir Edward Hillary failed to capture or sight Abominable Snowman, seen by father of Hillary's Sherpa guide, Tenzing Norgay (insert).

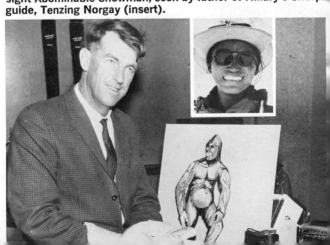

Five years after Patterson photographed Bigfoot (above), group of men in Pacific Northwest took photo of same or similar creature.

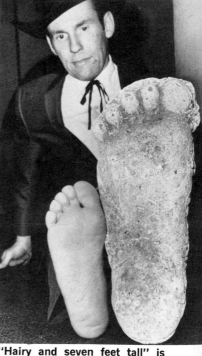

"Hairy and seven feet tall" is Roger Patterson's description of Bigfoot. Patterson compares his foot with cast he says he made of monster's footprint.

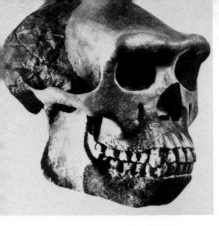

PEKING MAN
restoration of skull

Christopher Janus holds photo supplied by mystery woman on top of Empire State Building.

Unidentifiable marine animals washed ashore near Suez, Egypt in 1950 (above) and in 1970 at Scituate, Mass. Second creature was later found to be a basking shark.

THE BERMUDA TRIANGLE—GRAVEYARD OF SHIPS AND PLANES

1. Freighter *Sandra* sailed from Savannah for Venezuela—never heard from again . . .

2. British plane *Star Tiger* radioed its position, then mysteriously disappeared . . .

3. British airliner departed for Chile with 20 aboard—and vanished . . .

4. Five torpedo planes on training flight never returned. PBM rescue plane with 13 aboard also was lost . . .

5. Plane carrying 32 flew 100 miles toward Miami—never arrived . . .

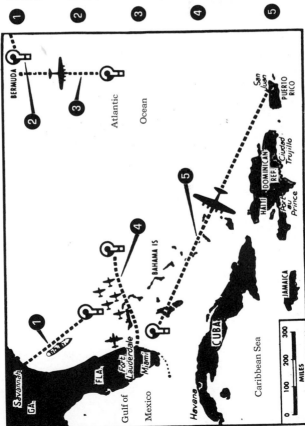

Eastern Airlines pilots Whitted (l.) and Chiles claim to have seen wingless monster similar to the above flying saucer.

Flipper of 30-foot creature was filmed in Loch Ness, Scotland, according to Robert H. Rines, president of the Academy of Applied Science.

Satanism and witchcraft are practiced throughout the world. Anton LaVey founded the Church of Satan in San Francisco.

Despite exorcism rite by Rev. Peter Vincent (l.), Michael Taylor savagely killed wife.

Strange creatures have suddenly appeared from Biblical times to present-day. Photo shows one that startled people in Huntsville, Alabama.

Mystery of 16-ton Easter Island monoliths and other ancient relics may point to presence of visitors from distant planets.

monster is a nocturnal animal), and even set off a number of blasting charges in 1963 in an attempt to recreate the conditions which brought Nessie to the surface in 1933 and 1934. Perhaps the explosions worked. There were another 40 recorded sightings that summer. A year later the number dropped to 18.

In 1966, Americans got into the act. Dr. Roy Mackal, a biochemist from the University of Chicago, came to the lake for a long, hard look. His theory was that Nessie was some kind of giant sea-slug with gills. His idea was cautiously aired in the world's scientific journals.

The first sonar probes took place in 1968. A team from the University of Birmingham set up operations on a Loch Ness pier, beaming high-frequency sound waves through the water. During one 13-minute sounding, the sonar echoes defined massive moving objects. Not one, but two. A Birmingham spokesman announced that the echoes were "clearly" made by animals.

A year later, two new techniques were tried. A British television network anchored a balloon over the lake. Attached to the balloon was a time-lapse camera designed to take periodic pictures of the lake surface. Nothing came of it.

The second new technique used in that summer of 1969 was the introduction of a submarine. Another American, this time oceanographer Don Taylor, brought a small scientific submarine to the lake, intending to chase the monster down and photograph it at close quarters. He went away shortly thereafter without having accomplished anything. No one had bothered to tell him that visibility in the dark waters of the loch was limited to about 12 inches.

"Why not infared, then?" reasoned Americans who returned in 1970 for another try. Infared film, which reacts to heat rather than light, might succeed in the murky waters. But nothing came of this venture either.

Another American group, the Boston-based Academy of Applied Sciences, also went to the lake in 1970. And again in 1971. Then once more in 1972. The first two summers produced nothing, in spite of a patient nightly watch on the waters of the loch, probing the depths with the very latest in underwater camera equipment and sophisticated sonar gear. But in 1972, the Bostonians (in cooperation with the lake's own LNPIB) connected. In the early dark hours of August 8, 1972, the sonar gear suddenly pinpointed something lumbering along under 45 feet of water. It held steady for a few minutes, then disappeared.

Robert Rines, an M.I.T. physics graduate who led the Boston team, had his jubilant men stand ready. Sure enough, a few minutes later the echoes pinged again. The creature, if that's what it was, had returned. Rines and his team followed it, then lost it again. Not to be denied, Rines pulled an old fisherman's trick. He had searchlights shined into the water, hoping to attract whatever was down there. It worked! The sonar tracings started up again.

When the evidence was examined later by experts back in the United States, the results indicated that the sonar had picked up two Nessies, creatures that were at least 20 to 30 feet long, with humps on their backs, long tails and fins.

Skeptical scientists were not convinced by the Boston team's findings. Maybe they picked up signs of living creatures, maybe they didn't. If the monster exists, doubters say, it must eat. And while there are fish and eel in the lake by the millions, ample to feed two or three of the giant creatures, there would hardly be enough to feed 20 or 30. And that's how many would be needed to constitute a breeding herd of Nessies.

Meanwhile, the search goes on. Something is out

there, the believers insist. There have been too many sightings, too many "proofs." If Rines's sonar didn't pick up echoes from a living thing, they ask, then what was it?

Only Nessie knows the answer. And Nessie, if she exists, is apparently too shy to come up and settle the question once and for all.

Nessie is the most popular figure in a wide array of water-bound whatsits, but she isn't the only one. Mentioned before was her sister, splashing through the waters of Lake Champlain. But Nessie's American counterpart hasn't been given a catchy name, nor is she as easy to locate, since Lake Champlain offers so much more hiding space in its 107-mile length. Consequently, the American Nessie has never captured her equal share of front-page headlines.

And what of sea serpents who have the entire length, breadth and depth of the oceans in which to hide? They take many forms, according to startled eyewitnesses. There was the giant stingray, more than 50 feet across from fin-tip to fin-tip, which reportedly took on the freighter *Lewis Luckenbach* for a two-day battle in Mexican waters. There was a 30-foot seagoing beast with a bright red neck ruff and eyes like dinner plates that surfaced briefly off the Scottish coast in the thirties. Closer to home, there was a one-horned sea monster, approximately the size of a runaway truck, which supposedly thrashed its way down Arkansas's White River past a whole collection of astounded picnickers.

One creature which stuck around for a longer look was the thing which washed up on a Tasmanian beach off Australia in 1960, following a raging storm. It was described as some kind of huge, fur-covered mass roughly 20 feet in diameter. Dubbed the "Tasmanian Thing" by gawking onlookers, it was unlike any known creature. No scientist was able to identify it. And they had plenty of time to try. It stayed on the beach for a year before authorities finally blew it up to get rid of it.

But the most puzzling of all sea monsters is not a creature at all. It is a sea itself, a horrifyingly unpredictable stretch of water known as the Bermuda Triangle.

Chapter Seven

THE BERMUDA TRIANGLE

You're a flight controller at Fort Lauderdale Naval Air Station. You've just come on duty in the control tower. It's a typical south Florida winter day outside— variable winds, clear skies, bright sunshine. There is a light chill in the air, but nothing comparable to the winters up north.

You check off the flight schedules before you settle down to work. Training flights, cargo arrivals, a transport due later that afternoon with new recruits. Nothing out of the ordinary. Routine.

You pour yourself a cup of coffee, wishing you had traded shifts with someone. Christmas is only three weeks away, and you still have a lot of shopping to do. As always, you'll probably goof around and wait until the last minute to do it.

Then the control-tower radio crackles to life with the first of a series of puzzling and frightening messages which will blot all thoughts of Christmas from your mind.

"Hello, tower," the radio says. "This is Flight 19. We seem to have an emergency here. We appear to be off course. We can't see land. Repeat, we can't see land."

There is tension in the voice, but you know that the first duty of a flight controller is to remain calm. You flip quickly through your log of flight schedules, checking to see who's talking. Lieutenant Charles C. Taylor of Corpus Christi, Texas, is listed as the leader of Flight 19. It must be Taylor on the radio.

Even as you're looking up this data, you have picked up the tower microphone and you're saying, "What is your position, Flight 19?"

"We're not sure," the voice says. "We can't be sure where we are. We seem to be lost."

Lost? In the middle of a bright sunshiny day? You check your log again. Flight 19 is supposed to be a routine training mission. Five of the rugged little Navy TBMs—the stubby torpedo bomber known as the "Avenger" when it was sinking Japanese battleships during World War Two. The five planes were supposed to head out over the Atlantic and zero in on a target ship anchored below Bimini in the Bahamas. Then, after they made their practice torpedo runs on the target hulk, they were to regroup and run through some navigational exercises.

But now they're in trouble? That could be dangerous. Three men in each of the planes, except for Marine Lieutenant Forest Gerber's plane. His gunner took sick at the last minute and stayed behind. That meant 14 men out there, apparently lost.

"Assume a bearing due west," you tell the planes crisply. "You'll spot land very shortly."

"We don't know which way west is," the voice says. It sounds confused, edging toward frantic. "Everything is wrong. Strange. We can't be sure of our direction. Even the ocean doesn't look right."

You sink into a chair by the radio, your stomach tied in knots. Suddenly all those old sea stories come back to you. The Hoodoo Sea. The devil's own playground. Can they be true?

You swallow hard and lift the microphone. "Listen," you say, trying to sound confident. "Don't panic. Hold on. Help is on the way. I'm calling for a rescue plane right now. We'll have someone out to you in a matter of minutes."

It is December 5, 1945, just four months after the end of World War Two. And Flight 19 has just flown into what is commonly regarded as the world's most fearful geographical monster—the deadly Bermuda Triangle.

If one stretches one's imagination from Miami at the tip of Florida, north to the Bermuda Islands, then south beyond Puerto Rico and back to Miami, one gets a roughly triangular patch of water which has mysteriously claimed the lives of more than a thousand sailors, fliers and passengers, most of them since the end of World War Two.

The heavily trafficked Bermuda Triangle is an open sea filled with sudden waterspouts and baffling streaks of "white water." It has reached out for unsuspecting travelers and dragged them into limbo without leaving a trace almost since the day it was discovered by Columbus and his intrepid band of seamen. No one will ever know how many men were lost before puzzled mariners started keeping count of the vanished victims.

It's a tricky area. The rapid Gulf Stream current sweeps through it. There are deep, unexplored canyons running through the floor of the Atlantic beneath it. There are violent weather patterns, storms that blow up from nowhere and abate just as swiftly. Furthermore, it's one of the only two stretches of ocean on earth where a compass needle points to true north, rather than to magnetic north. (The other treacherous area where this compass variation plagues seafaring men is "The Devil's Sea," an equally deadly expanse of water in the Pacific, southeast of Japan.)

Large and small boats, some 60 in number, have disappeared forever, without leaving the slightest trace.

Planes, more than 40, have vanished. Small wonder that the area has struck travelers with fear and earned a variety of names, all flavored with mystery and danger. Some call it the Devil's Triangle. Others call it the Hoodoo Sea, Triangle of Death, Graveyard of the Atlantic. Even early Spanish sailors called it the Isle of Devils. Explorer Sebastian Cabot, preparing his map of the area in 1544, named it *"Ya de Demonios"* (Place of the Demons).

Whatever you call the treacherous triangle, it exists. And no one has yet been able to explain it. A number of theories have been developed: Flying saucers, hovering in space, whisking the victims away to giant zoos in the sky. Mysterious mechanisms on the lost continent Atlantis, still being triggered by passing vessels and aircraft. Even that there is some unknown civilization, advanced and extremely powerful, living beneath the Atlantic, pulling passengers down for closer scientific study.

Ridiculous? Perhaps. But return to that day in December, 1945, when you are still listening to Flight 19, wondering with increasing alarm what is happening to those five lost planes.

The first message came at 3:45 P.M. Now it is 40 minutes later. For a while you could hear them talking. They obviously have each other in sight. They've been talking back and forth, trying to figure out what has gone wrong.

You've already notified the Banana River Naval Air Station, about 150 miles up the Florida coast, and they've dispatched a big Martin Mariner PBM flying boat on a search and rescue mission, just in case.

About 4 P.M., you heard Lieutenant Taylor turn his command over to one of the other planes, but you don't know why. Now the radio crackles again. It's Marine Captain George Stivers, the new flight leader.

He says, "We're still not sure where we are. We think we must be about 225 miles northeast of base."

You grab the microphone. "Flight 19, this is Fort Lauderdale tower. Can you read me?"

There is no answer. Only static. Then the voice says, "It looks like we're entering white water."

"Come in, Flight 19," you say. "This is Fort Lauderdale tower. Please acknowledge."

A broken voice comes on. Not Stivers. One of the others. It says, "We're completely lost."

Then there is silence.

It is the last message anyone will ever receive from Flight 19!

In the meantime, the Martin Mariner is winging toward the last assumed position of the missing flight of torpedo planes. The Mariner, a huge flying boat with a crack crew of 13 trained search-and-rescue men, is prepared to do everything possible to pick up the missing men if they have been forced down. The Mariner is equipped with self-inflating rafts, waterproofed radios, food, everything the men might need if they have been downed. Further, the Mariner carries enough gas to keep her looking for more than 24 hours if necessary.

Within a half-hour, the Mariner reports that she has reached the position, but can see nothing. No planes. No wreckage. Nothing. A little later, the Mariner sends another position report.

It is the last word from the rescue plane!

The Mariner, with her crew of 13, also vanishes.

As soon as contact with the rescue plane is lost, the Navy and Coast Guard rush into the search with every plane and vessel on the coast of Florida that can be spared. Nearly 300 planes and 19 ships join the search mission, the most intensive search and rescue mission ever undertaken. The ships and planes scour an area of over 280,000 square miles for five days. But they find nothing. They find no debris. They find no oil slick. They find no survivors.

Twenty-seven men and six planes have disappeared from the face of the earth, never to be seen again.

The roll call of the Bermuda Triangle's victims stretches back through seafaring history. One of the first recorded mysteries was that of the French ship *Rosalie,* found drifting lifelessly in the Bahamas in 1840 with its sails set, its cargo untouched, no apparent signs of trouble, but its crew vanished. In 1880, a British training frigate with a crew of 290, the *Atalanta,* sailed for Bermuda and disappeared. This was the first disappearance to attract wide attention, due in part to the fact that a number of her crew were young British naval cadets.

One of the largest ships ever to vanish in the triangle was *U. S. S. Cyclops,* a 500-foot American coaling ship that sailed into the area March 4, 1918, with a crew of 309 men. The *Cyclops,* on her way from Barbados to Virginia, left no slick, no debris or other trace. Since World War One was still going on at the time, officials first thought she might have been sunk by a German U-boat, but a search of German Admiralty records after the war revealed that no U-boats had been in the waters of the West Indies at that time.

More recently, the 425-foot freighter *Marine Sulphur Queen* disappeared off the Dry Tortugas with all hands. That was in 1963. Smaller craft include an American yacht, the *Connemara IV,* lost in 1955; the ocean racing yawl *Revonqc* and the cabin cruiser *Witchcraft,* both of which dropped out of sight in 1967, and a Norwegian freighter, the *Anita,* which came to grief in 1973.

Not to mention a whole fleet of airplanes. For example, before the five TBMs of the ill-fated Flight 19 and the Mariner flying boat disappeared, another Navy plane, a PB-4YW, had flown into the area with a crew of 15, never to fly out again. That was July 18, 1945. Two years later, on July 3, 1947, an American C-54 Superfort tested the area and, like the others, also vanished, this time without broadcasting any word of difficulty.

Nor have the victims always been military planes. On January 30, 1948, a luxury British airliner, the *Star Tiger*, a four-engine Avro Tudor IV, disappeared over the triangle with 31 passengers and crew aboard. A year later, the *Star Tiger*'s sister plane, another Tudor IV called the *Star Ariel*, vanished en route to Jamaica with 18 aboard. Search missions for both failed to turn up any wreckage. Through the next two decades, planes continued to disappear—a Navy Super-Constellation in 1954, a Navy Martin P5M seaplane in 1956, a KB-50 Air Force refueling tanker in 1962, a C-119 Flying Boxcar in 1965.

Perhaps even stranger than the thin-air vanishing act of ships and planes are the numerous ghost ships which have been encountered in the triangle, floating craft with only one thing missing—the crew.

Ghost ships have haunted the imaginations of sea going men since the birth of the *Flying Dutchman* legend. The *Dutchman*, a sailing ship out of Holland, supposedly ran afoul of supernatural powers in the middle of the Seventeenth Century when her irascible skipper, Captain Vanderdecken, cursed in anger when confronted by an avenging angel (or perhaps even God Himself), fired his pistol at the apparition and blasphemed. The apparition laid a curse on him, condemning him to sail the high seas throughout eternity, alone and without rest until the end of time. The moment the curse was uttered, the crew and the passengers of the *Dutchman* disappeared, and the captain, assisted by no one but a demon cabin boy, has ranged the seas ever since, slipping back and forth between this dimension and others, plaguing honest, God-fearing seamen by appearing at moments of danger.

But the ghost ships of the Bermuda Triangle have no captains or demon cabin boys. There have been no survivors at all.

Some of the silent, drifting ghost ships have been brought to port. In addition to the French ghost *Rosalie,* already mentioned, another, the *Mary Celeste,* was first sighted in 1872 by a British barkentine, the *Del Gratia.* There was some weather damage evident on the *Mary Celeste,* and a few feet of water in her bilges, but nothing to show why her crew might have abandoned ship. The *Del Gratia* placed a prize crew aboard the *Mary Celeste* and brought her into Gibraltar. No one ever determined what happened to the crew.

More recent ghost ships include the *Carroll A. Deering,* found crewless in 1921, and a two-masted schooner called the *City Belle,* which was located about 300 miles southeast of Miami in 1946, minus her crew of 32 men.

Undoubtedly, the most hair-raising ghost ship experience ever to come out of the triangle is the strange sight which appeared before the captain and crew of the cargo ship *Ellen Austin* in 1881.

The *Ellen Austin,* sailing halfway between the Bahamas and Bermuda, came out of poor weather, becalmed and drifting, within sight of another schooner that apparently was suffering from the same lack of sailing wind. The two ships drifted within sight of each other for several days before they drew close enough for hailing. It was the morning of August 20, 1881, when the captain of the *Ellen Austin,* a man named Baker, took up his hailing horn.

"Ahoy there," Captain Baker called. "Who are you?"

There was no answer.

The ship was quite still, sails faintly luffing in the wind. Her two dories were still lashed down above the main cabin, and a galley door banged restlessly in

83

the quiet as the schooner rocked gently in the swells. But there was no sign of life aboard.

Captain Baker decided to investigate. He took his first mate, Stanley Moore, and a few of his own crewmen and rowed over in a dory to inspect the listless ship. They clambered aboard and took a quick look. No one. Not a single living creature. The cargo was still there, a load of mahogany.

"A good prize, Cap'n," Moore said.

Captain Baker nodded. After all, the law of the sea says an abandoned ship goes to the man who can bring her in. But even sea captains are not immune to the superstitions common to sailors, and Baker didn't like the feel of this too-quiet ship.

"I can feel wind in the air, Cap'n," Moore insisted. "Time might be short."

Baker made his decision. He quickly ordered a prize crew to take charge.

Sure enough, the breeze came up before midnight, and the two schooners decided to put about and head for Boston. Two days later the wind increased and reached almost gale intensity, bringing wind squalls. The two schooners lost sight of each other during the storm, but on the third day, when the storm abated and the dawn broke cool and calm, the *Ellen Austin* managed to relocate the prize ship standing off the larboard stern. But something was wrong. The decks were too still. Sails unattended. Navigational lights had apparently burned dry, perhaps explaining why the *Ellen Austin* and her crew had lost sight of their companions the night before.

Captain Baker tried hailing her, but it was the same as the first day. No answer. He called for the dory to be lowered again and rowed over for another look.

The mate, Moore, watched uneasily from the *Ellen Austin,* and he was standing by when a grim-faced Captain Baker returned.

"Well, sir?" Moore asked.

"Everything was just as before," Baker said slowly. "The cargo is still intact, no signs of trouble. But now the prize crew is missing."

Baker assigned Moore to head another prize crew. Moore asked hesitantly to be relieved of the duty, and the crew grumbled, but Baker had become stubbornly insistent that the prize be brought to port and to his pocket. Moore and the others went along, the mate looking sorry that he had ever even suggested bringing in the ghost ship. No one argues with a sea captain, at least not for long. To refuse to obey a captain's orders at high sea is mutiny, a hanging offense. So they left the *Ellen Austin* and rowed over to the derelict.

Once more the two schooners set off for port. This time Moore and the prize crew were ordered to ring the ship's bell every 15 minutes, day and night. Captain Baker was taking no chances on the same thing happening to his second prize crew.

On the second day after the new crew took over, the prize ship drifted into a sudden fog bank. The ship was no more than a dozen ship lengths behind when the fog bank appeared. The bell stopped ringing. The *Ellen Austin* hove to and fired several rounds in an attempt to make contact. There was no answer.

"Put about!" a panicky Captain Baker ordered his second mate. The *Ellen Austin* sailed back to the approximate location where the prize ship had disappeared into the fog bank. There was nothing there.

The mahogany-laden prize ship was never seen again. Nor was either of the two prize crews, nor the original crew. Captain Baker and his schooner returned to port in complete bafflement.

What are the Navy and Coast Guard attitudes toward the mysterious disappearances that are still going on in the Bermuda Triangle? Officially, the U. S. Navy

85

refuses to recognize the triangle as a danger zone. Many Navy spokesmen maintain that the triangle is no more prone to inexplicable disappearances than other heavily trafficked ocean regions. They point to the Devil's Sea, off Japan, and the Sable Triangle, an area stretching from Sable Island off Nova Scotia to the Azores and up to Iceland.

The Coast Guard responds readily to inquiries about the mysteries of the Bermuda Triangle, but it insists that most of the disappearances can be traced to what they call "the area's unique environmental features." The Coast Guard has even prepared a pamphlet which offers rational explanations for the oddities in the area —freak weather storms in which violent winds and rain squalls mature suddenly and abruptly over the warm water in the triangle; mechanical failures; the magnetic anomalies of the area in which compasses suddenly seem to go crazy; and, to explain the otherwise unexplainable, the old standby, human error. As the pamphlet says, "The combined forces of nature and the unpredictability of mankind outdo even the most farfetched science fiction many times each year."

There have been other explanations over the years. In 1921, after the *Carroll A. Deering* was found crewless and adrift off North Carolina, the daughter of the missing captain, a Miss Lulu Wormwell, sent a telegram to a U. S. senator indicating she had important information relating to "piracy on the high seas."

Why did she suspect piracy? For one thing, a man named Christopher Ray had reported a month earlier that he had found a message in a bottle near his beach home in North Carolina. The message was unsigned, but it said:

"*Deering* captured by oil-burning boat, taking off everything, capturing crew. No chance to escape. Finder please notify owners of *Deering*."

Miss Wormwell, armed with knowledge of the note,

contacted the firm which owned the derelict schooner and told them that she intended to press for a government investigation of the crew's disappearance and a close examination of her "piracy" theory.

Carroll A. Deering, for whom the ill-fated schooner had been named, responded favorably to her suggestion. Piracy would be easy, he acknowledged. At least in theory. Since few people would even suspect that pirates still sailed the seas, it would be possible for a band of determined men to carry on in the area without discovery for a very long time, particularly if the circumstances were right.

Other ship owners quickly agreed. Perhaps old-fashioned piracy had been resurrected. Perhaps modern cutthroats were ripping off the shipping industry right off the coast of the United States! That could explain the disappearances of crews, as in the case of the *Carroll A. Deering,* and it would go a long way toward explaining how entire ships had vanished without a trace.

Furthermore, they had another fillip to add to the growing piracy theory: politically inspired pirates, working directly for a foreign government. The 1920s were the Red Scare days. A number of "experts" theorized that the pirates were Communist zealots, seizing ships on the high seas and taking them to Soviet Russia.

Most ship owners rejected the idea. It was extremely unlikely, they said, that modern pirates could have pounced on so many ships without the facts leaking out. Ships even in those days, they pointed out, were nearly all equipped with wireless radios, and the chances of their being seized without a distress message getting out were quite slim. Furthermore, the ships could hardly be pressed into service elsewhere under another country's flag without being recognized, no matter how well they might have been disguised. Even

87

if the plan was to offload the cargoes and sink the ships, the stolen cargoes would still have to be landed somewhere and sold if the pirates were to profit from their crime.

As for the message in the bottle which started this newest flurry of piracy tales, government investigators compared it with Christopher Ray's handwriting and determined that he had written it himself. Confronted with this evidence, Ray admitted that the note had not come from the *Carroll A. Deering*. He claimed that fishermen near his home had come up with the idea as a joke. The bottle and the government investigation of Twentieth-Century piracy were quickly laid to rest. The fate of the *Carroll A. Deering* remains a mystery.

At least the piracy theory convinced more people than many of the recent popular theories about flying saucers and lost Atlantis mechanisms and unknown underwater civilizations. These theories have popped up in many recent books on the triangle, such as the national bestseller by Charles Berlitz, grandson of the founder of the famous Berlitz language school. Berlitz explores many of the peculiar theories about the triangle—the "zoo probes" from outer space, the "machinery-gone-wild" in lost Atlantis, the unknown "super race" living deep in the earth. He even suggests that the missing ships and planes may have been slurped up by "magnetic vortices" which are somehow linked with "a different point in time and space." Some of the theories he cites led a Harvard historian, Samuel Eliot Morison, who has sailed the Bermuda area himself, to challenge them publicly. "The book is preposterous," snorts Morison. "Almost all hooey."

Is it hooey? Are there forces at work in our oceans which no amount of rational thought will ever explain? Can unknown intelligences be sucking people into the sky, labeling them and stuffing them into cages for an interstellar ride back to some distant planetary zoo?

For a consideration of that we must turn our speculations to a whole new breed of monsters, the silver-skinned creatures who began to invade our skies and our attention during the famous flying-saucer flap of recent decades.

Chapter Eight

UNIDENTIFIED FLYING WHATSITS

It was late afternoon on October 11, 1973, in Pascagoula, Mississippi. A couple of Mississippi shipyard workers decided to go down to the pier by the old grain elevator for a little night catfishing on the Pascagoula River, and walked smack into one of the weirdest UFO contacts ever reported to authorities.

The two men were Charles Hickson, 45, and Calvin Parker, 19. All they wanted was a quiet evening, filled with the simple pleasures of staring at the water, maybe pulling in a few hardheads or redfish, some casual conversation, then home to bed.

It was getting on toward dusk when they arrived. A big, orange sun was drifting through the dusty haze toward the horizon. Fish *plipped* on the surface of the river after low-flying insects. Charlie Hickson, a balding, quiet man, pulled out his tackle and settled down on the banks. His young friend, Calvin, a farm boy with dark hair and sideburns, hunkered down beside him.

By the time night fell, they had a couple of bullhead catfish to show for their efforts and the conversation had turned to Jones County where young Calvin lived. Hickson had come from Jones County, too. He owned a house and farm up there, and nights like this were a good time to talk of home.

Then suddenly, out over the water, a strange blue light appeared. Both men stopped talking right away. As Hickson said later, "You're really surprised when you look up in the sky and you see a blue light. It kind of calls your attention to it."

The light hovered for a moment, then started floating across the river toward them. At first neither man knew what to make of it, but as it kept getting closer it began to take shape in the darkness. It appeared to be some kind of machine—a humming spaceship shaped like a giant cigar.

Young Calvin went hysterical. "Oh, oh, oh," he moaned. And for good reason if we are to believe the story the two men told later. For the craft paused in front of them, floating a few feet off the ground, going *nnnnnnnn, nnnnnnnn,* and a door opened up in its side. Three wrinkle-skinned creatures with big eyes and pointed ears came drifting out of the doorway and floated, not walked, toward them. As the three creatures drew closer, the two shipyard workers could see narrow little mouths without lips and hands like crab claws.

Calvin fainted. On the spot. His older friend, Charlie, scared half to death, started to cry. One of the creatures glided up to him and began to make soft buzzing noises, as though trying to reassure him that nothing would hurt him or his friend.

Although still in stark fear, Charlie got at least partial control of himself. He stood his ground, watching the trio of "invaders." They bobbed about him, looking him over; then one of them reached out with its crab-claw and touched him.

Apparently Charlie became weightless after the touch. He says two of the creatures took him by the arms and guided him, floating, across the surface of the water and into the spaceship.

There were no seats inside, at least not seats as we

know them. Only some kind of large glass eye fixed to the cabin wall which scanned Charlie from head to foot. And all the time, as Charlie whimpered, the creature kept buzzing at him. Finally, apparently satisfied with the results of the examination, the creatures floated Charlie back outside and deposited him on the river bank. Then the glowing ship throbbed a few times and swished off into the night.

Hogwash? Maybe a little too much moonshine in the moonlight? Authorities wondered the same thing when Charlie and Calvin came to them with the story. Charlie's wife and his employers at the shipyard said he was a "reasonable" man, not given to wild stories or heavy drinking or the like. Both Charlie and Calvin claimed they had not been drinking at all at the time of the encounter, though they admitted they had gone quickly for a drink or two after it was over, "to settle our nerves."

There were at least a few believers. Dr. J. Allen Hynek, an astronomer from Northwestern University, quickly flew to Pascagoula after news reports of the incident and questioned the two men under time-regression hypnosis. Hynek, satisfied that the two men were telling the truth, said later, "There's simply no question in my mind that these men have had a very real, frightening experience. It was just like an aborigine who sees his first 747."

Charlie Hickson also took a lie detector test. An experienced polygraph operator gave him a clean bill of health: "Hickson told the truth. He believes he saw a spaceship. He believes he was taken aboard a spaceship. He believes he saw three space creatures."

It would be easier to shrug off Charlie's and Calvin's experience if it weren't for the existence of a long history of unexplained encounters with so-called Unidentified Flying Objects. And the Pascagoula encounter wasn't an isolated incident. There were other sightings

91

in Mississippi that same night, and that same month in 1973, reports of spaceship sightings came flooding in from all over the country. The governor of Ohio, John Gilligan, driving through Michigan with his wife, was startled to see some kind of strange craft made of amber light. It stayed in the air above him for about 35 minutes. A park ranger in Mississippi reported seeing a saucer-shaped craft with blinking red, green and yellow lights. A group of sheriff's deputies chased across the Louisiana countryside after a flight of five amber-colored UFOs until one of the deputies made the mistake of flashing his red lights at them. Then the five craft turned around and came down for a closer look, scaring the deputy stiff. When he turned off his lights, they took off in a flash and vanished. Then there were as many as 150 citizens of Columbus, Ohio, who reported watching a formation of pulsing lights zipping through the night skies. There were 2,150 UFO reports in 1973 alone.

Why the sudden resurgence of spaceship sightings?

Strange shapes in the sky had been a big thing in the years following World War Two. Scarcely a day passed that someone didn't look up and see a saucer, or a cylinder, or a set of pulsing lights. But those days had all but passed. The authorities made such a fuss about it, dismissing most of the sightings as hoaxes and hallucinations, that it took a pretty thick-skinned individual to pipe up and admit he had seen anything. Such an admission invited instant derision, mockery, laughter. It was easier to look the other way and forget about it.

Yet, when a Gallup poll was conducted in 1973 on the subject of UFOs, the results indicated that at least 15,000,000 Americans could claim they had seen one. That's 15,000,000. One out of every 13 men, women and children. Next time you get on a bus, take a look around. If there are as many as 30 people on the bus, chances are at least two of them have looked into the sky and choked back the surprise as something "unknown" whisked overhead.

The same poll indicated that 51% of the population of this country, asked if they believe that UFOs are real, would answer firmly, "I do." Fifty-one percent. That's more than 102,000,000!

Things in the sky aren't new. Even before the rash of sightings following World War Two, history and ancient literature record an impressive number of strange goings-on in the earth's atmosphere. Perhaps the earliest such record is the one carved in granite on a mountainside in China's Hunan Province. Some ancient artist, amazed at what he had seen or heard about from others, chipped away at the granite until he had recorded the vision—large creatures with thick chests, while above them, perched on cylinder-shaped objects, other creatures looked down from the sky. Scientists have dated these carvings at somewhere around 45,000 B.C.

There are many such prehistoric allusions to visitors from the sky—carvings, figures, cave-paintings, religious myths. But we shall deal with them more fully in the next chapter. For now, let's stick to less ancient history. For example, the Nineteenth Century. There was a flurry of sightings in the late 1800s. Two sons of the Prince of Wales, one of them destined to become a king of England, looked up from the deck of a ship between Melbourne and Sidney, Australia, in 1881 and reported seeing some great shape which looked to them "like a fully illuminated ship." Americans saw similar craft in 1897. All the way from Chicago to Benton, Texas, came reports of enormous flying objects which seemed to have fins at both ends.

The Swedes got their first modern look at strange craft in 1933, when a number of "planes" were reported flying through the dangerous mountain regions

93

without bothering to land for refueling. These were the so-called "ghost fliers" of Sweden.

Then, in World War Two, came another kind of aerial intervention. U.S. combat pilots kept reporting a kind of fireball which came flying up on them and followed them wherever they went, as though playing tag with them. Dubbed "foo fighters" by Allied pilots, it was thought that these orange and red balls were some kind of German secret weapon, designed to disrupt our radar and screw up our electrical systems. After the war, though, we learned that the Germans had also been plagued by "foo fighters," and they thought it was an Allied secret weapon.

Next came the "ghost rockets." In the summer and fall of 1946, a year after the war, a whole bevy of cylindrical objects were observed in the skies of Europe, orange flames shooting from their tails. Western authorities suspected the Russians, convinced they were carrying out rocket tests with missiles captured after the fall of Peenemünde. The Russians denied it.

By now the stage was set for the modern wave of "saucer reports." It began quietly enough on August 1, 1946, when Captain Jack Puckett, U.S. Tactical Air Command, was headed toward MacDill Air Force Base in Florida in a twin-engined C-47. Something whisked across the sky ahead of him and he had to bank sharply to avoid hitting it. At first he thought it was a meteor, but then he got a closer look. According to the report he made after landing, it was "a long, cylindrical shape, approximately twice the size of a B-29 bomber, with luminous portholes."

Puckett's sighting wasn't the one that started the saucer craze, but it was the first in this country. It was followed by a number of scattered reports through the remainder of that year and into the next. But the report that sent the nation into a tizzy of excitement was the one that came on June 24, 1947. This time a civilian pilot, a young businessman named Kenneth Arnold, was winging along above Mount Ranier in Washington when he suddenly spotted nine silvery disks whipping through the air at very high speed, flying in formation. Arnold, shaken, headed for the ground. He reported what he had seen—or thought he had seen—and made history by referring to the nine vessels as "saucer-shaped." Newspapers snapped at the story and the term "Flying Saucers" was born.

Saucer fever swept the world. Sightings occurred almost everywhere, until eventually there were 70 countries on the list. There were reports from pilots, ground sightings from civilians, photos, burned places where saucers had supposedly set down. Many of the reports were undoubtedly hoaxes, others were mistakes—weather balloons, flights of geese, optical illusions. But there were enough solid reports from apparently expert witnesses to make military blood run cold. Was something really out there? Did the Russians have some new air technology we didn't know about? The reports, reliable or not, were enough to send military intelligence people into a complete dither.

Nor were all the sightings peaceful ones. On January 7, 1948, a state trooper in Kentucky spotted some kind of giant object in the sky and promptly called Goodman Air Base to report it. The commanding officer of the base, Colonel Guy Hix, contacted three P-51 fighters flying in the area and asked them to take a look. The lead pilot of the P-51 flight, Captain Thomas Mantell, was about to begin a chase which would cost him his life.

Mantell, a seasoned pilot who had fought in the skies of North Africa and Europe during World War Two, led his men to the coordinates given him by Goodman tower. He soon spotted the object and reported that it was traveling half his speed and was directly ahead and above him.

95

"Can you give us a description?" the tower asked.

A few moments passed, then Mantell said, "Yes, tower. It appears to be metallic and tremendous in size."

Moments later, Mantell was on the radio again. He said, "I'm at 10,000 feet and pursuing the object. It's going up and forward now as fast as I am. I'll pursue it as high as 20,000 feet."

None of the three P-51 pilots was equipped with oxygen, and so 20,000 feet was dangerous. Mantell obviously knew this, but something he had seen lured him on. The other two pilots, in the meantime, leveled off at 15,000 feet and started back down.

Nothing more was heard from Mantell. Two hours later, the wreckage of his plane was found scattered over a three-mile area.

The Air Force spent a year and a half investigating the incident, then announced that Mantell had probably blacked out at a high altitude from lack of oxygen, *while pursuing the planet Venus!*

A few months after Mantell died, two more experienced airmen encountered something out there. In July of 1948, Eastern Air Lines pilots C. S. Chiles and J. B. Whitted, flying over Georgia in a DC-3, spotted a "torpedo-shaped object about 100 feet long, with two rows of brightly lit windows along the side." It had no wings. According to Chiles, "Whatever it was, it flashed down toward us, and we veered off to the left. It veered off, too, and passed about 700 feet to our right and a little above us. Then it pulled up with a burst of flame from the rear and zoomed into the clouds."

Because it was early morning, most of the passengers were asleep when the encounter took place. But one who was not, a man named Clarence McKelvie, also saw it. He described it as looking like "a cigar with cherry flame going out the back."

96

It was sightings such as these, plus the death of Mantell and numerous other reports over American military air bases, that began to make the air intelligence people nervous. They came up with a classified report on the situation in which they suggested the UFOs might be of interplanetary origin. The report was bucked upwards all the way to Air Force Chief of Staff Hoyt Vandenberg. Vandenberg rejected it.

But the Air Force wasn't finished with UFOs. Reports continued to pour in that couldn't be ignored. The intelligence people, based at Wright-Patterson Air Force Base in Ohio, reorganized their UFO research under the name Project Grudge (perhaps miffed because their earlier report had been rejected). It was later to be known as Project Blue Book, a book which wasn't to close for 22 years.

The CIA was brought into the picture in 1952, after a rash of UFO sightings over Washington, D.C. The "extraterrestrial" beings, if that's who they were, were getting far too cheeky. In July of that year, F-94 jet interceptors were called up again and again to chase "objects" out of the restricted air corridors over the nation's capital. On the night of July 19, radarscopes at National Airport tracked seven unidentified objects. Nobody knew what they were, nor exactly where they were, but every time the interceptors took off to chase them, they vanished at speeds estimated to be as high as 7,000 miles per hour. Then, as soon as the jets came back to base, the blips reappeared on the radar and zipped around in the skies above Washington until the jets took off again. This game of space tag lasted almost six hours.

A week later, on July 27, there was a repeat performance. Not only in Washington, but across the country. It was enough to scare the oldest of hands in the capital. Congressional demands for explanations reddened Air Force faces, since the Air Force didn't have any answers. In addition, the Korean War was then still underway, the Russians had just set off their first H-bomb, and security people were in a tizzy. Were the UFOs a threat to security? Could it be some kind of Communist ploy? A propaganda scheme? Something to make us look like a nation of war-crazy nuts?

Because of the Washington sightings, the CIA stepped in and gathered a group of top scientists to analyze the UFO phenomenon. Called the Robertson Panel after their head man, Dr. H. P. Robertson, a physicist from the California Institute of Technology, the scientists focused on the fact that the UFO reports were causing a great deal of trouble, jamming phone lines with saucer reports, cultivating a dangerous national hysteria. Authorities apparently became convinced there was only one thing to do. Put the saucers back on the kitchen shelves where they belonged. Debunk the whole idea.

That's when the ridicule started. From that point on, Project Blue Book people started downgrading reports, even when they came from reliable witnesses. Military personnel were easy to handle. No ridicule for them. Instead, they were slapped with a gag rule which made the public release of any information on UFOs punishable by a fine of $10,000, and up to 10 years in a military stockade. Small wonder, then, that UFO reports diminished in quantity and quality over the next few years.

An example of what happened to men who were willing to go against the new Air Force position on unidentified flying objects is the treatment handed to American Airlines pilot Peter Killian. Captain Killian and his first officer, John Dee, were at the controls of a DC-6 over Pennsylvania in February of 1959. Out of the darkness came three huge disk-shaped objects, flying in formation. The three intruding craft flew along beside Killian's plane for several minutes. Brightly lighted, the craft kept pace with the plane, then put on speed and disappeared in the darkness. Not only did Killian and his copilot see the three craft, but so did the passengers.

Shortly after Killian told newspaper reporters what he had seen, the Air Force stepped in and explained that Killian had actually seen three stars, not three spacecraft. Killian stuck to his story. They weren't stars, he said. They were disk-shaped objects, just as he had reported, and they had flown beside his plane. His copilot backed him up, as did several of the passengers. The Air Force scoffed at his story publicly.

The argument grew bitter. Killian had his reputation and his professional standing at stake. If he was so blind that he couldn't tell the difference between stars and disk-shaped objects right outside his cockpit window, then he had no business flying. And if his eyesight was okay, then the Air Force was casting doubt on his honesty.

The argument reached the halls of Congress, and concerned congressmen suggested Killian be given a chance to state his position before a House Committee. The Air Force backed off. Yes, okay, they said. It wasn't stars that Killian saw. Instead, it was the lights of three jet bombers and a refueling tanker.

The argument ended abruptly. Killian still had reason to argue. An experienced pilot shouldn't have that much trouble telling the difference between a refueling flight of standard aircraft and three so-called UFOs. But he kept quiet. A spokesman of the National Investigation Committee of Aerial Phenomena (NICAP) later announced that Killian's wife had come to NICAP with the story that American Airlines had muzzled him, forbidding him to continue the public discussion. She said the Air Force had pressured the airline.

Then, on September 13, 1965, a new group of sightings hit the headlines. Police Sergeant Eugene Bertrand, in Exeter, New Hampshire, came across a distraught woman behind the wheel of a car parked under an overpass. He told her to move on, that she was obstructing traffic and her car constituted a traffic hazard. She refused to budge, though, and poured out a story of fear. A giant thing, flashing red lights, had chased her down the highway for 10 miles; then when she sought refuge under the overpass, it had swerved away above the woods.

Sergeant Bertrand thought he had a real nut on his hands until he got back in the patrol car and switched on his radio. Then he heard a fellow patrolman on the air talking about finding a man with a story just like the woman's. A giant glowing object had chased him until he took cover in a ditch.

The sergeant hurried out to join his colleague for a look at the area where the young man had been found cowering. On his way, he passed a farm field in which a number of horses were galloping about wildly, as though scared half out of their wits. When he reached the open field and saw the other patrol car, he pulled up and asked what had happened. He got the same story over again, a giant red thing, floating through the air. He had about decided that the young man and the woman both had only seen a helicopter or something, when suddenly he saw it himself. The whole field lit up, bathed in a red glow, and a vaguely round-shaped object dropped over the field and paused, hovering silently about a hundred feet above the ground.

It was enormous, maybe 80 feet or so in diameter, and it was ringed with a band of flashing red lights. The two policemen and the young man who had already seen it one too many times stood at the edge of the field, quaking, until the giant object began to move away. Sergeant Bertrand immediately notified Pease Air Force Base. While he was talking with officials at Pease, half a dozen other residents of the area called in to report seeing the big, silent red form. Two of these later witnesses were driving on the road and reported that the shape passed only a few feet above them, forcing them to stop their cars.

Following this new saucer publicity, two things happened rather quickly. First, the Air Force announced that the explanation for the Exeter sightings was simple, that the "eyewitnesses" had simply come up against weather balloons—either one or several—in the area. Many of these balloons are quite large, they explained, and are often equipped with running lights.

Next, after two decades of investigating UFOs and encountering nothing but cynicism from one side or the other, no matter which course they took, the Air Force investigators decided to get out of the business and put the controversial Project Blue Book to rest for all time. In October, 1966, the Air Force turned the UFO problem over to a scientist from the University of Colorado, Dr. Edward U. Condon. His assignment: study the cases listed in Project Blue Book objectively and come to a conclusion, once and for all, about the value of the so-called UFO reports.

Condon might have been a welcome arbiter if it had not been for a slip of the scientific tongue three months later. Speaking before a gathering of his scientific colleagues, Condon said: "It is my inclination right now to recommend that the government get out of this business. My attitude right now is that there's nothing in it." Then, with a quick smile, he added, "But I'm not supposed to reach a conclusion for another year."

It took Condon and his team two years to produce a massive 900-page document titled *Scientific Study of Unidentified Flying Objects*. The gist of the document was outlined on the first page—that nothing had come of the study of UFOs in the past 21 years which added anything of substance to scientific knowledge.

The Air Force promptly announced that Project Blue

Book was officially closed. The files and photographs and evidence from over 12,000 UFO sightings (Condon and his team had looked closely at only 90 cases) were packed and stored under lock and key. UFOs were declared an unworthy subject for continued investigation.

The National Academy of Sciences seconded the Condon report by saying that 90% of the sightings could be easily explained as mistaken glimpses of earthly aircraft, weather balloons, space hardware and satellites from our own earth missions, and an accumulation of gases, heat lightning and other natural phenomena.

That left 10% remaining as not so easily explained, but in fairness to the official point of view, it must be remembered that UFOs present to science much the same problem as Bigfoot creatures—they have consistently refrained from leaving hard evidence behind them. Given the wreckage of a saucer or two, with maybe a few corpses from a downed UFO, science would have solid evidence to analyze, and perhaps new conclusions would be reached. It is difficult to give credence to the popular theory that government and scientific bogeymen deliberately suppress all "evidence" of extraterrestrial visitors, if only because in a nation filled with good investigative reporters and curious scientists, not to mention the unknown quantity of international spies, it has proved difficult to suppress *anything* the government would just as soon not become public.

However, newspapers also seemed to lose interest after the Condon report. UFO sightings became a topic not worth covering. The 20-year-old flying saucer flap had ended.

But the saucers refused to cooperate.

Reports dropped off for a while, perhaps because the inevitable nut element in the population, which had been seeing extraterrestrial beings every time a cloud sailed overhead, crawled back into the woodwork. What was the point in seeing strange sights if no one would listen to you? The Air Force had closed up shop. Newspapers generally turned a deaf ear. Neighbors laughed if you brought it up. But the solid citizens who were convinced they'd seen something were still disturbed. Non-believers have a tendency to become believers quickly when they see a thing they can't possibly explain.

Then the UFO fuss heated up again. After what amounted to a three-year layoff, the unexplained visitations seemed to pick up speed in 1972. Newspapers noticed the commotion and began to carry the stories again. Not the big play they had given the subject in years past, but isolated stories here and there. A floating light in Florida. A hovering object in Texas. A cylinder in California. And the witnesses were the kind one might ordinarily consider reliable. Police officers in Wittenberg and Montello, Wisconsin. Traffic cops in Galion, Ohio. Sheriff's deputies in Gem, Kansas. More policemen in Wheaton, Illinois. And even newsmen. An aerospace writer from Chicago. A newspaper photographer from Cape May, New Jersey, In all, more than a thousand new UFO reports rippled through the public consciousness in the summer and fall of 1972.

That was only a prelude to the avalanche of reports in 1973. After the Pascagoula experience of Charlie Hickson and Calvin Parker, the sky seemed to turn dark with unidentified missiles. Reports started cropping up all over the country. Visual sightings, blips on radar screens, shapes whooshing from horizon to horizon. It was as though saucers had been reborn, although some long-time saucer experts maintained that it was not the saucers making a reappearance, but only a measure of respectability which allowed witnesses to speak out who might otherwise have kept quiet. The saucers were never gone, the saucer-philes told us. They were there, even in the quiet years.

As might be expected, the new public attention to

103

UFO phenomena also brought out the hoaxers. Just outside the city limits of Dayton, Ohio, motorists were shocked when they saw two "space creatures" in silver suits cavorting through the trees, their long antennae bobbing cheerfully as they dashed from bush to bush. Police quickly responded to calls and found two young Dayton schoolboys who had wrapped their bodies with rolls of aluminum foil and had attached silvered coat-hangers to their heads. The police were not amused.

It is well for us to consider the hoaxes along with natural mistakes, hysterical conclusion-jumping and downright lies when considering UFO sightings. Pure numbers don't always count. As the National Academy of Sciences had suggested back in 1969, perhaps 90% of the UFO sightings *can* be explained away simply. That would mean as many as 1,000 of the 1973 reports were probably faulty. But we're still left to puzzle over the other 250.

There is, of course, the definite possibility that all the reports will be explainable someday, maybe the next time there is another big rash of saucer reports. The variety of puzzling phenomena which defy scientific explanation at the moment might turn out to be caused by some presently unknown, but perfectly harmless, natural force.

Then again, they might not.

Chapter Nine

GODS AND MONSTERS FROM OUTER SPACE

If saucers from other worlds really have been visiting earth for the past 25 years, why did they wait so long before they came to look us over?

The answer, if you're willing to believe a chubby pop hero from Switzerland, is that they didn't. Rather, extraterrestrial beings have been using earth as a commuter stop for untold thousands of years, and the evidence is here to be seen.

Erich von Däniken, a stocky Swiss writer with an impish smile, produced a book in 1969 which was to become a cult classic. His *Chariot of the Gods?*, produced first in German, then in English, has gone through 44 paperback printings and has sold more than 5,000,000 copies, making him an instant hero to people around the world. The success of his book has opened the field to imitators, and now it's almost impossible to go into a bookstore without seeing at least a dozen titles that suggest God was an astronaut from another star system.

Von Däniken's ideas aren't new. He admits this himself, between trips to the bank. As a matter of fact, the plaudits for this theory should probably go to a Russian physicist named Agrest, whose hypothesis that visitors came to our planet from a distant star and left a number of unexplained extraterrestrial monuments was published in 1961, eight years ahead of von Däniken. But even Professor Agrest doesn't really deserve full credit. Imaginative science-fiction writers have been playing for years with the theme that Adam and Eve were space travelers, marooned on earth when their rocket stripped its gears and parked for repairs in the Garden of Eden.

Nevertheless, von Däniken popularized the theme. He took a number of literary and mythical references from our historical heritage and speculated that this planet has been visited and explored at least twice by super-intelligent, non-terrestrial races. According to him, they came to earth in prehistoric times and made themselves at home, passing out gifts of wisdom and civilization which may help explain some of our more

105

puzzling earthbound monuments—the pyramids in Egypt, the massive carvings on the plains of Nazca in Peru, the giant stone monoliths on Easter Island, ad infinitum. On occasion, von Däniken theorizes, visitors from other worlds acted less than gentlemenly, mating with earthlings, blowing up the biblical cities of Sodom and Gomorrah in an early version of the A-bomb explosion at Hiroshima, and causing the great flood which sent Noah scrambling to the nearest woodpile for the makings of the Ark.

What possible basis could von Däniken have had for such an eye-popping set of speculations? It might not be so far-fetched. Let's take a look at some of the "evidence."

First, dismiss the geocentricity which allows us to think of ourselves as the only living beings in the universe. Current scientific thinking offers us a figure of something like 250 billion star systems in our galaxy alone (and the number of comparable galaxies in the infinity of the universe is a figure beyond thinking). Okay, so we have 250 billion star systems in our own small corner of the sky, the milky way. Of those 250 billion stars, scientists speculate that perhaps half have planetary systems similar to our own. That's 125 billion planetary systems. Still, to be cautious, pare the number down some more.

Let's agree with a more conservative scientific estimate that perhaps eight billion of those planetary systems in our galaxy are capable of producing life in some form. Not necessarily intelligent life, but life. Of those eight billion, let's say that only one in a thousand systems has a planet which has developed intelligent life—rudimentary intelligence, perhaps lower-order animals, slugs that feel simple impulses, moss that registers hunger and cold. That narrows us down to eight million planets.

Go a step farther and say that one in a thousand planets with living creatures on it has developed in a

106

somewhat parallel manner with earth, going slightly beyond rudimentary intelligence, perhaps even developing speech and primitive civilization. That still leaves us with 8,000 planets out there, trying to grow up. Now let's take the last step. Say that only one in a thousand of these earth-type planets goes beyond simple civilization and develops a higher order capable of space flight and super intelligence. That means there are eight super planets, perhaps competing with each other for their share of dominance in the milky way, watching us in amusement the way we might watch a colony of monkeys in a local zoo. And at the same time, hoping there isn't a super-super intelligence on some neighboring galaxy that might consider them as primitive as they undoubtedly consider us.

Still sound like too many super races in our own galaxy? Stop and briefly re-think the numbers. Eight billion planetary systems which scientists think are capable of producing life. That's an eight followed by nine zeros—8,000,000,000. We're wiping out the zeros, all nine of them, and taking the most cautious possible estimate (short of sticking to the ridiculous assumption that we are unique, the only intelligent beings in the entire universe). We are saying that even if only one out of a billion planets capable of producing a higher life form has done so, there are still eight of them out there.

And it only takes one.

With that numbers game in the back of our minds, let's look at von Däniken's evidence, if it can be called that. Remember, he derived it from others; so go beyond von Däniken and pick it up from the original sources, just to make sure he hasn't been playing the old shell game on us.

To start with the plains of Nazca, this is a desert wasteland near the coast of Peru. The area is hard and rocky, and crisscrossed with shallow indentations, including straight, wide footpaths which strike off in this

107

direction and that, here stopping short for no discernible reason, there disappearing into the distant heat shimmer.

Archaeologists had noticed these troughs or paths while seeking information on the ancient culture of the Incas, but they usually dismissed them as being Incan roads that seemed to go nowhere.

Then in 1941, Dr. Paul Kosok, a history professor from Long Island University, flew over the plains on his way to an appointment in Lima and discovered the lines were not just lines. He ordered another plane to return to the area for aerial photographs. The pictures that resulted show squares, triangles, enormous figures of whales, spiders, monkeys, crabs and a number of geometric doodles startling in their precision.

Perhaps these giant carvings lend themselves to a simple explanation. It is a well-documented fact that pre-Columbian civilizations had risen to sophisticated heights in such fields as astronomy and engineering. Furthermore, any contemporary college freshman who has ever worked in a card section at a football game knows that a small diagram can easily be enlarged to flash "Go Bobcats!" in letters 50 feet high.

But cultists ask, who put the Nazca carvings there? Any why? More important, how? The lines are thought to have been etched into the rock facing by a pre-Incan civilization, but how did they manage without flying above the area to check the results? And since the figures mean nothing to earthbound people, why bother even if they did have the engineering ability?

Not far away, on the face of a red cliff in the Bay of Pisco, is another figure, a giant trident, some 820 feet high, visible for a distance of many miles, pointing inland. Landing instructions for a prehistoric space bus? A directional signal for an anticipated space rescue mission, like "Help" stamped out in the sand?

Similarly, there are unexplained stone heads on Easter Island. The first European explorers to land on the island, back in the 1700s, were astonished to find hundreds of massive stone carvings, some weighing as much as 50 tons, chipped out of house-high chunks of volcanic rock. Easter Island is more than 2,000 miles from the coast of Chile, the nearest mainland. No one knows who carved these colossal heads, nor how they managed without machinery to transport them from inland deposits of volcanic rock on the island to their silent resting places on the island's coast.

Norwegian archaeologist Thor Heyerdahl has proposed a theory, itself a fascinating scientific whodunit, that early inhabitants of the island erected the statues themselves solely with primitive tools, reed floats and extraordinary patience; but advocates of the ancient-visitation belief are convinced that an early civilization erected the figures to honor strange beings who had dropped in for a visit, using techniques they learned from the visitors and which have since been lost in the cobwebs of man's short memory span.

One can point to all sorts of monoliths, godlike carvings, non-rusting iron shafts, man-made objects that appeared thousands of years before the technology to create them is known to have come into being. They are scattered through our ancient cultures, in South America, India, the Yucatan peninsula, Egypt. One can visit museums and see what appear to be working models of electric batteries which are thousands of years old, quartz beads which bear tiny holes for stringing which some theorists think couldn't have been made by anything but the most recent commercial drills, writings which contain numbers of 15 digits, small gold ornaments which look like delta-winged jet fighters of today, ancient calendars which break our terrestrial year down into 365.2420 days, more accurate even than the calendar we use today (though we have refined the earth year figure to 365.2422 days).

Then there are such mysteries as the Piri Reis maps.

In 1513 Piri Reis, a noted Turkish admiral, found some ancient maps and used them to make copies of his own. The maps were forgotten over the years, but in 1929 a scholar poking around in the Topkapi Palace in Constantinople found the yellowed Piri Reis charts. He was astonished to discover that the charts contained what appeared to be a rough outline of North and South America. Since the map was dated only 22 years after Columbus discovered the new world, it seemed to be an excellent find. True, the charts appeared to be somewhat distorted, but the shapes weren't that far off.

The maps were put in the hands of an American cartographer for examination. Arlington Mallery, the recognized expert on ancient maps, agreed that the maps contained the proper geographical data, but he too was worried that everything seemed to be in the wrong place. So he sought the help of the U.S. Hydrographic Office and the Western Observatory in Boston.

Mallery, with assistance, constructed a grid system and transposed the Piri Reis markings to a globe. The results were little short of astounding. Not only did the map suddenly become accurate, it also contained data on Antarctica, which hadn't been discovered until 1819! Okay, consider the possibility of a hoax. The Piri Reis maps, though dated 1513, had been out of sight until 1929. Suppose some map hoaxer had planted them to delude modern cartographers. He could have drawn Antarctica with accuracy, could he not? Wrong. The map contained topographical markings—mountain ranges, rivers, plains, plateaus, all drawn with disquieting accuracy. These markings included a mountain range in the Antarctic which wasn't discovered until 1952! We've only barely finished mapping them ourselves, with the aid of echo-sounding gear.

Where did the Piri Reis maps come from? Some say outer space. Compare them with space photographs from high-flying camera satellites. If you place the camera above Cairo and shoot straight down, you will get a fairly accurate duplicate of the Piri Reis charts, with minor variations. Does that boggle the mind?

If not, consider the case of the corroded bronze artifact dredged up by sponge divers off the coast of Greece at the turn of the century. Cultists of the ancient-visitation theory tell us it is a 2,000-year-old computer, a kind of pre-Christian planetarium.

The "planetarium" was located by Greek divers off the coast of Antikythera in a sunken hulk which had lain there for 20 centuries. Among the statues and plates and ancient coins recovered from the ship was a hunk of ancient corroded bronze with brass parts. No one knew what it was, so it was unceremoniously deposited in a storage room of the Greek National Museum.

The mysterious hunk of metal remained in the store-room until 1959, when a Princeton scholar, Dr. Derek Price, ran across it and began to study it. He soon discovered that it was a calculating machine of some kind. There were sheets of bronze with markings replicating our solar system—the earth, sun, moon, planets. When one turned a miniature crank, gears and cogs revolved and brought the planets to their correct positions. In effect, the little machine gave remarkably accurate astronomical information.

But the Greeks of antiquity weren't known to possess any such machinery. Cultists theorize that the ancient Greeks got a close look at a more sophisticated planetarium device and tried to imitate it. The question becomes—whose planetarium were they imitating?

Clues pointing to ancient visitations crop up in all sorts of religious myths, we are told. Bear in mind that the following examples result from extreme simplification of complex religious systems, but consider: Eskimos believe that their forebears were brought to the frigid north by gods with metal wings. American Nava-

111

jos regard themselves as Earth Surface People, sub-
servient to powerful and mysterious predecessors who
once traveled about on sunbeams and lightning. Tibet-
ans, in their oldest writings, referred to flying machines,
calling them "pearls in the sky." The Aztec god,
Quetzalcoatl, was a strange man who came out of the
rising sun and taught the Aztecs science, arts and wisdom. When he was done, he sailed off to the east to
meet a ship which was to take him to the morning star.

Cultists also send us to the Bible whenever possible.
They seem convinced that the Bible is one of the most
fabulous UFO books ever written, filled with descriptions of pillars of fire, strange lights, chariots in the sky,
atomic holocausts, visitations from the hosts of heav-
en, wheels within wheels, clouds that hovered in the sky
to lead the Israelites out of the wilderness.

One of the cult favorites is the prophet Ezekiel, who
they say describes an encounter with a spaceship. The
encounter begins: *"As I looked, behold a stormy wind
came out of the north, and a great cloud, with bright-
ness round about it, and fire flashing forth continually,
and in the midst of the fire, as it were gleaming bronze.
And from the midst of it came the likeness of four living
creatures. And this was their appearance: They had the
form of men."*

Josef Blumrich, a NASA engineer, was so moved by
the cultist interpretation of the writings of Ezekiel that
he wrote a book about it. Called *The Spaceships of
Ezekiel,* Blumrich's book analyzes each biblical pas-
sage dealing with Ezekiel's encounter and offers technology to support it, including diagrams and illustra-
tions to complement some of Ezekiel's more abstruse
observations.

Ezekiel tells us, *"Their legs were straight, and the
soles of their feet were round; and they sparkled like
burnished bronze."* Sound like gold-anodized space
suits? Or the legs of a soft-landing module? You can

112

have your choice. There are a number of popular interpretations to choose from.

The prophet also tells us: *"Over the heads of the living creatures there was the likeness of a firmament, shining like rock crystal, spread out above their heads."* The dome of a spaceship? A space helmet? And also, *"When they went, they went in any of their four directions without turning as they went. The four wheels had rims; and their rims were full of eyes roundabout."* Wheels with openings, as one might find in a mesh? Or wheels with bulging protuberances, like stumpy spikes? Ezekiel doesn't make it very clear. But either would work to help a vehicle move in desert terrain. Then, *"When the living creatures went, the wheels went beside them; and when the living creatures rose from the earth, the wheels rose."* Of course. Ah, Ezekiel, what have you done to us?

These visitors from outer space went too far from time to time. Another of the visitors-from-space writers, Brinsley Le Poer Trench, who wrote *The Sky People* in 1960, suggests that the expulsion of humanity from the Garden of Eden came because some of the early visitors mated with earthlings and infuriated the galactic spaceman-in-chief. He points to Genesis 6: 1–2 as his basis for this belief: *"And it came to pass, when men began to multiply on the face of the earth, and daughters were born unto them, that the sons of God saw the daughters of men and they were fair; and they took them wives of all they chose."* Trench goes a little far, though. He also suggests that the original Garden of Eden was not on earth, but on Mars, and that the Great Flood was what ended the Mars colony. The escape vehicle was Noah's Ark, not a boat at all, but a giant spaceship.

Von Däniken also likes to think of the biblical God and his angels as being intemperate space visitors, capable of losing mortal tempers and raining super-technological death from the skies. He points to the catastrophe of Sodom and Gomorrah as evidence. Two "angels" came to visit Abraham's brother, Lot, and were greatly disturbed when the local townspeople, a surly and evil group of citizens, according to the Bible, tried to "know" them sexually. The angels struck the offenders blind and told Lot to gather up his family and get out of town, as it was to be destroyed. When Lot balked, the angels took him in hand and virtually dragged him from the city, telling him to hurry, to *"escape for thy life; look not behind thee, neither stay thou in the plain; escape to the mountain, lest thou be consumed."*

Von Däniken says the haste implies a countdown, an irrevocable act that couldn't be recalled. He suggests that Lot and his family were being hurried to get them away from ground-zero, and that the rain of brimstone and fire which destroyed the two cities of Sodom and Gomorrah were much the same as the two bombs that destroyed Hiroshima and Nagasaki. Which might explain why Lot's wife, who disobeyed the angels and stopped and looked straight into the atomic holocaust, was struck dead instantly.

There's more. The prophet Elijah, after accusing King Ahaziah of blasphemy, was set upon by one of the king's men and 50 soldiers who had been sent to arrest him. Elijah called down "fire from heaven," which wiped out all 51 men. A second group sent by the king met the same fate. A third group was a little smarter. When they saw what had happened to the first two groups, they begged for mercy and were allowed to live. Cultists ask if this "fire from heaven" doesn't sound like some kind of laser-beam attack from a protecting UFO circling overhead. To add fuel to this particular fire, they point out that Elijah, after the death of King Ahaziah, took off in a "whirlwind into heaven." Think of a rocket or a saucer or a helicopter or any of the other flying vehicles we know today taking off from a

114

dusty desert floor. Wouldn't it look like a whirlwind?

One final biblical point, though there are many others which appear in the literature of the ancient-astronaut cult. Remember the story of the Ark of the Covenant which Moses constructed according to directions from above? God told Moses just how everything was to be fitted, from what metals and alloys it was to be made, everything. No mistakes would be countenanced. Then the Ark was to be put away, with only selected individuals allowed to come near it to speak to God; and God even gave instructions as to the kind of clothing and footwear these intermediaries were to wear. No one was ever to touch the Ark, that was made quite explicit. But generations later there was a slip-up. In the time of David, the Ark was being moved. As the cart bobbed along, carrying the Ark to its new home, the cart threatened to overturn. A man named Uzzah reached out quickly to steady the Ark. Even though he was trying to help, acting faithfully to protect God's "instrument," he was struck dead on the spot, as though struck by a lightning bolt.

What does this have to do with supposed ancient visitations from outer space? Easy. The Ark, according to the disciples of von Däniken, was a communications device. In effect it *was* a lightning bolt that struck Uzzah down. The Ark was electrically charged.

One might expect Bible scholars to be enraged by the twists given to the scriptures by UFO cultists. Many are. Many believe in only the strictest reading and interpretation of holy writings. Others, more liberal in their attitudes, remind us that God works in mysterious ways. They contend that the Bible is not necessarily out of step with science *or* fantasy. As long as one is willing to accept the results on faith.

Rev. Barry Downing, in his book *The Bible and Flying Saucers*, says biblical religion might be the deliberate work of beings from another world. He says:

115

"If beings from another world had contact with our world, isn't it possible they were more concerned to give us a morality, and an understanding of the purpose of life, than to help us make a few technological advances?"

But the ancient-astronaut theorists have other enemies, even in the field of science. Dr. Carl Sagan, the Cornell University astronomer who designed and placed an extraterrestrial message in the form of a plaque on NASA's Pioneer 10 space probe, believes firmly in the possibility that extraterrestrial life exists, but holds a dim view of von Däniken and his predecessors and imitators.

Sagan, speaking before the American Astronautical Society, once said, "The earth may have been visited by various galactic civilizations many times during geological time. It is not out of the question that artifacts of these visits still exist, or even that some kind of base is maintained within the solar system to provide continuity for successive expeditions."

But when faced with some of the more outlandish of the von Däniken theories, Sagan bristles. Von Däniken was careless with his facts, Sagan suggests, misquoting experts (including Sagan himself), shuffling inaccuracies from shell to shell in a kind of cosmic shell game. All of the artifacts put forward in *Chariot of the Gods?*, Sagan claims, have a variety of "plausible, alternative explanations."

He uses the plains of Nazca as an example. If people believe in the existence of gods in the sky, as most cultures do, why is it so difficult to understand the markings on the Peruvian plains? The markings may well be, in Sagan's words, a "collective graphical prayer." Their presence in the rocky plain is evidence only of those who uttered the prayer, not necessarily evidence of the reality of an intended recipient of the prayer.

Whatever one might think of the von Däniken speculations and the rocky ground on which he has, like the ancient inhabitants of the Nazca plains, built them,

116

scientists today generally recognize the almost certain probability that life exists elsewhere. Further, most scientists reject the chauvinist attitude that ours is the only advanced culture. Indeed, our culture is probably quite primitive in that its development has thus far taken place in what might amount to only a blink in time compared with the unfathomable eons which have gone into the creation of the universe. It's as though a race of gnats, newly arisen since the invention of DDT, looked about them and said, "We are the chosen people, the only ones."

Someday, the inventors of DDT might come back with a new gnat squasher.

Chapter Ten

MONSTERS OF THE MIND

On March 25, 1975, a jury filed back into the courtroom at Leeds Crown Court in England and delivered a verdict in a tragic murder trial, a trial filled with accounts of witchcraft, demonic possession and supernatural violence so horrifying in its intensity that court officials said it reminded them of the blackest excesses of the Middle Ages.

The crime? Michael Taylor, a tall, thin, 31-year-old unemployed British farm laborer of limited education, stumbled out of a Barnsley church in October, 1974, shivering and exhausted after undergoing a seven-hour, all-night exorcism ritual during which he had seen 40 of his own "personal devils" cast out by two British clergymen. Two hours later he attacked his wife at home and, convinced that she too was possessed by devils, murdered her quickly but bloodily with his bare hands.

The verdict? The English jury, after hearing the

bizarre testimony regarding Michael Taylor's gradual decline into the pit of demons, the subsequent rites of clerical exorcism in which he participated and the incredible act which he committed only hours later, found him not guilty by reason of insanity. The judge ordered him sent to Broadmoor Prison for the insane.

Taylor's slide into the dark netherworld of demons and Satanic possession is only one aspect of the modern wave of fascination with the occult which has swept the world in the last 20 years. Not many of us have flown over the plains of Nazca and wondered if we were looking down at a message to space-suited gods. Not many of us have climbed a high, snowy pass in the Himalayas and shiveringly wondered, "Yeti?" as we gazed upon mysterious tracks. But many of us have confronted monsters in our own minds.

Old beliefs die hard, even in this modern age of skepticism. Today, you will find serious people involved in complex occult and psychic arenas stretching from black magic all the way to the edges of the "white magic" of science, such as the extrasensory-perception experiment in which astronaut Edgar Mitchell attempted to communicate thought to earth from Apollo 14.

Michael Taylor's path was bleak all the way, but it started innocently enough. Happily married to Christine Taylor, the 29-year-old "darling of his life," Taylor had a great deal going for him. He had five young sons, a devoted wife, loving parents, a good job on a northern English farm. But the economic crunch came along and his life began to slip away from him.

It could have happened to anyone. First he lost his job. A man without work is a man without a paycheck, and with a wife and five children to support, the walls begin to close in quickly. Taylor tried to find work, but there just weren't any jobs open. He fell into a state of depression, watching his wife and sons trying to make do on the little they had.

Taylor turned to religion for comfort. He began attending meetings of a religious organization called the Christian Fellowship Group, a fundamentalist sect which normally gathered for Bible readings and hymn singing in the homes of members.

At one of these meetings, Taylor's feverish attention was caught when he saw one of the members of the sect administer the rites of Holy Communion to another member, then fall into a fit of religious fervor and begin "speaking in tongues," a state which borders on hysteria and involves the utterance of a string of unintelligible sounds, which are regarded as fragments of prayer in an unknown language. The religious zealot who had caught Taylor's eye claimed to be possessed by the Holy Spirit.

Taylor sat quietly in his corner of the living room, mesmerized by the heat of the worshiper's religious fanaticism. As if that were not enough, the "possessed" worshiper then performed an act of exorcism on another participant in the group, casting out a demon. That did it. The ritual of exorcism had a profound effect on Taylor. He left the meeting in an irrational state, claiming he had seen the devil as it departed from the exorcised member of the prayer group.

For the next several days, Taylor's condition worsened. He demanded that his wife remove all crosses and religious material from their home. He began to behave violently. Friends worried about him. They finally took him to the Anglican St. Thomas's Church in the Yorkshire hamlet of Gawber to see the Reverend Peter Vincent, 52-year-old vicar of the church. But Taylor flew into a rage and struck one of his friends who had taken part in the Christian Fellowship meetings. Reverend Vincent's wife, who witnessed the sud-

119

den rage and attack, later said, "There was an enormous force of evil emanating from Taylor."

The Reverend Vincent, concerned at what he had seen, sought the advice and help of a Methodist minister in the area, Reverend Raymond Smith. Together, they decided Taylor might well be demonically possessed by Satan, by some strong force of evil which would react to nothing but some prolonged rite of exorcism.

On the evening of October 5, 1974, Taylor was brought back to the Gawber vicarage where the two ministers, Vincent and Smith, along with three other men, worked long and hard to relieve him of his private demons. They worked all night, casting out demon after demon, 40 in all, according to trial testimony; but when they had finished, there were still three demons left—insanity, violence and murder.

The men involved in the exorcism realized when the all-night vigil ended that they had not fully succeeded. As Taylor left them, they worried that what he needed most might well be psychiatric help. They tried to contact authorities, but it was too late.

Taylor carried his remaining demons home and confronted his wife. She knew something was wrong. She tried to talk to him, tried to soothe him, but nothing worked. She slipped from the house briefly and went to a neighbor seeking help. They called for a doctor, but when Christine Taylor went home to wait for the doctor to appear, she walked into the dark pit of Michael Taylor's personal obsession. She, too, was possessed, he told her. She was filled with the devil and it must be rooted out. Before she could do anything, say anything to set his mind at ease, he seized her and clawed at her. The details that came out in court are too grisly to repeat, but the result of the attack, as prosecutor Geoffrey Baker was to say later at the trial, was that Mrs. Taylor died rapidly from inhalation of blood.

Citizens and authorities in Taylor's small English

town were horrified by the crime. Devils and exorcism? How could it have happened? Who was to blame? The religious group which first set him off? The two ministers and their three assistants who had tried to help Taylor by the rite of exorcism? Taylor's mental state? Or were there really devils, over which mortal man has no control?

Taylor cast his own finger of guilt. After his arrest, he told police that it was the unwitting fault of the men who performed the exorcism on him. "They tried to bring me peace of mind," he said, "but instead they filled me with the devil. I was compelled by the forces within me to destroy everything in our house."

Others apparently agreed to some extent. Canon John Pearce-Higgins of the Church of England was incensed. "The blasted meddlers will dabble about in demonism," he said, "not knowing what they are doing or what might happen. The damage it can do is immeasurable."

The Right Reverend Eric Treacy, Anglican bishop of the Wakefield diocese where the ritual took place, also spoke up. "I am bound to say that the attempts at exorcism during the night before the murder were unwise. No clergyman in the diocese of Wakefield has my specific authority to practice exorcism. But I am aware that some clergymen will feel that it is a normal part of their pastoral ministry when occasion demands."

In spite of the overwhelming popularity of modern films such as *The Exorcist,* one does not readily expect to see contemporary examples of possession, Satanic impulses, cleansing rituals, or any of the hundreds of other occult entries in a black book filled with supernatural gifts, powers and curses. That belongs in the darkness of the Middle Ages, right?

Wrong. The demonic lies barely beneath the surface. Scratch the average person with a tale of ghosts, witchcraft, spiritualism, ESP, reincarnation or what have you, and he'll probably have an equally hair-raising tale to spin back at you. Usually these stories are told in fun, with a proper dash of cynicism. But you'd be surprised how often the cynicism masks a deep-seated fear that the stories might well be true, after all.

In fact, England underwent such a resurgence of old-fashioned witchcraft and supernatural dabbling in the early 1970s that one group of Anglican church authorities, meeting with top-level Roman Catholics, seriously recommended the appointment of official exorcists in every English diocese, just to keep pace with the demons who needed to be driven out.

Witchcraft and exorcism go together because possession is thought to be caused frequently by the black arts of witchcraft. Witches, at least some of them, in league with the forces of darkness, supposedly call down demons through the casting of spells and send them to do their worst, driving victims to acts of unspeakable vulgarity and blasphemy.

What happens when a person is possessed? The demon (or demons—they seem to favor working in teams) takes hold of the victim's psyche. Popular film treatment accurately follows the widely held opinion that the victim's face and body usually go through a startling variety of contortions, twisting into caricatures of evil, positions which are often thought impossible for an unpossessed person to duplicate. The voice changes to gruff, vile tones, screaming obscenities and dark blasphemies. Victims also, according to the possession stereotypes, foam at the mouth a lot, vomit all manner of strange items (broken glass, bits of wood, pins and needles, small pebbles), wail like animals, become incredibly strong, even float in the air.

Unbelievers, faced with the prospect of a screaming, cursing, wailing contortionist, have often identified the symptoms as common hysteria, or more uncommon attacks of epilepsy and similar muscular and mental afflictions.

But believers run for the church and the same cure that churchmen have used for centuries—the rites of exocism.

Exorcism, simply stated, is a hand-to-hand combat, a duel between priest and demon. The demon, if we are to believe the stories that have built up around these ceremonial battles, usually does its best to resist —mocking the priest and lying to him, spouting obscenities and irreligious invective, trying its best to distract the priest and to turn him away from his exorcism duties. If the priest is weak, the demon may well win. But if the priest is strong and faithful, the battle is joined. It may take many forms. It may involve the sprinkling of holy water, the touch of a crucifix or stole, the recitation of prayers and holy litanies (prayers are supposed to be quite painful to the demon). Exorcism is no preliminary event, limited to three quick rounds and a unanimous decision. It might go on for months. Even after the demon is expelled, there is always the danger he might return. Amateurs are warned to stay strictly away.

Not all aspects of the supernatural are painful or harmful, of course. Even among witches, there is a decided distinction. Black witches may invoke evil forces from the darker regions of nature (or supernature), intent on causing pain or malicious harm to enemies, but there are also "white" witches who use powers beneficially—to heal, to act as quieting influences in a world of turmoil, to achieve good.

Witchcraft is as old as antiquity. Its proponents claim that it is the oldest religion, beginning with the fertility rites and worship of nature gods by early man. According to a witchly variation of Biblical history, the first witch was Adam's first wife, Lilith. She was such a horror, mothering whole armies of demons, that Adam finally turned from her and married the gentler Eve. Lilith became a night visitor, one of the bugaboos with which mothers bribed their children into acquiescence ("You'd better be good, or Lilith will get you").

Witches really came into their own, however, during a frenzy of witch-hunting in the Fifteenth Century, when European churchmen decided they had to be put down. Witch hunts, complete with burnings at the stake, crushing with heavy rocks and boulders, crucifictions and boiling in oil, continued in Europe for the better part of 300 years, and finally migrated to Puritan New England in time for the famous Salem witch trials. All the witch hunts managed to accomplish, however, beyond the deaths of untold presumed witches, was to drive the practice of witchcraft firmly underground.

Nowadays it is easier to be a witch. Or at least to claim to be one. No one burns witches anymore. So it's easy enough, if desired, to operate openly. And many do.

During the height of the Vietnam War, hundreds of witches and border spiritualists in south Texas openly set up shop to help young Mexican-Americans avoid the draft. Charging anywhere from a pair of chickens to as much as $500, border witches put hexes on the Department of Defense, local draft boards and anything else which would help keep the young men out of uniform. It didn't always work. After all, it takes a heap of hexing to hold off the entire U. S. Army. But some young men swore by it. Even if they were ultimately drafted, they made second visits to make sure they would get home safely.

In Africa, a leading soccer team from Nairobi, Kenya, spent as much as $3,000 to make sure witches would help a winning season to continue. For fees of from 12 to 60 dollars a crack, the team approached witches before each match to seek advice and forecasts. In one game, the Nairobi team came up against another team that wasn't above using witchcraft, too. Officials from both teams stormed the stadium office and demanded that they be allowed to check the ball before game time to see if any charms had been placed on it.

In southern Italy, it is common for every village to have its own *stregone,* a witch skilled in the arts of casting and uncasting spells, healing diseases and driving away evil spirits, just as most Mexican villages have a *bruja* or a *curandero* for the same purposes.

Sure, Africa, southern Italy, the Texas border, Mexico—these are areas rich in folklore in which some inhabitants, particularly rural people, hold hard to the old ways. What about the cities? What about Paris? London? Tokyo? New York? Can there be witches in the midst of so-called urban "enlightenment"?

There certainly can. Come with us to a typical meeting of a witches' coven. It is Saturday night, the time of Black Mass. A young lawyer and his wife are waiting in their comfortable home in an expensive tract-housing development. The clock creeps toward midnight. On the door, welcoming the expected visitors, is a black-and-orange emblem, pitchforks crossed on a field of velvet.

The guests begin to arrive. They include an insurance salesman, a bank clerk, a postal employee, two housewives, a young sociology major from a nearby university. Twelve people in all, with a thirteenth who is recognized as leader.

They greet each other in friendly fashion, chatting inside the doorway, not much different than any group of young people about to share a few cocktails and an innocent game of charades.

But the charade they will soon enter is different. You can detect the difference the minute you get a look at the trappings in the room. There is an inverted pentagram on the wall, purple and emblazoned with a

125

green goat image. The sign of the Satanists. A skull rests on a black swath of cloth above the fireplace mantle, flanked by burning candles.

As the clock strikes 12, the young lawyer draws the drapes and members of his coven begin to strip off their clothes (becoming "sky-clad" in witches' parlance). When they are all nude, the men and woman join in a circle traced symbolically by a knife, facing outwards, and begin to dance in a spiral, chanting as they move.

The dance is awkward looking. The men keep their weight only on the toes of their left feet, giving them a peculiar jerky motion. At a precise moment in the ritual, the lawyer breaks the circle and leads the dancers inward in a spiral toward the center. When he reaches the middle of the ring, he starts back out to the original circle. The others follow. The circle is rejoined.

This double-spiral dance, an ancient symbol of reincarnation, continues while the high priest purifies the circle by swinging an incense burner in the center. There is also a ceremony it which salt and water are consecrated through the use of incense. When the dancing ends, Satan and his minions are invoked and the evening settles down to some serious spell-casting.

There is some evidence that the fad is now passing, but groups like this are still meeting all over the country, in Chicago, Los Angeles, New York. And in smaller towns. Open your phone book and check the Yellow Pages to see if there are any occult bookshops listed. If so, chances are that enough occultniks live in your town to support a few witches' covens of their own. Not that there is a necessary connection between occult bookstores and witches' covens. But where there are enough people with interest in the occult to keep a highly specialized bookstore from going broke, the odds are high that some of them are dabbling in the black arts.

Interest in the occult—the word generally denotes something mysterious, something beyond the range of ordinary knowledge—also includes the unknown laws which govern mental telepathy, precognition, astrology, reincarnation and spiritualism, which is the apparently mystical ability to communicate with those beyond the grave.

Although fraud is not unknown in any of the wide variety of occult interests, it has been particularly rampant in the area of spiritualism ever since deceased Americans first began learning how to rap on tables in the 1840s. From that point onward, the night has been filled with intellectual and financial frauds who will take advantage of troubled people by summoning up the same old "voices" and levitating globs of would-be protoplasm.

But in spite of the existence of frauds and hysterical nuts who are quick to mistake psychiatric problems for psychic phenomena, there are many questions about so-called occult occurrences which cannot be answered. It would be wrong to dismiss the entire field of psychic phenomena out of hand just because there is not, as yet, enough acceptable evidence accumulated under the bright light of the scientific laboratory.

And when and if—a very big if—science is able to proclaim that it now knows all, there will doubtlessly still be people who find mystery and mysticism a more fascinating alternate route. For them, devils and unnatural powers exist. Who can say, with certainty, that they are wrong?

Eight days after Michael Taylor, the man whose mind became possessed by personal demons, was found "innocent" of the crime of murder, a new supernatural thriller called "The Exorcism" opened on a London stage. In the play, a woman is supposedly possessed by the spirit of another woman who had starved to death centuries before. Beautiful Mary Ure, Scottish-

127

born stage and film actress, was chosen to play the part of the possessed woman. The role required her to collapse during the play and to die offstage.

"The Exorcism" opened April 2, 1975. Mary Ure played her part quite well. Critics didn't think much of the play, but they liked Miss Ure. One said her acting was the most dramatic and impressive moment in the entire performance. She was excellent in the role of the woman possessed.

The next day Mary Ure was found dead in her London apartment. The timing startled newsmen and the story was quickly trumpeted around the world, appearing in newspapers and newsmagazines on both sides of the Atlantic.

There were no suspicious circumstances surrounding her death, except that a mystery quickly developed as to how she had died. Her co-producer said he understood she had choked on something while eating and suffocated. Others said it was an apparent heart attack. Two weeks later a coroner's court offered still another version—Mary Ure had died of alcohol and barbiturate poisoning.

Was it that simple? Some of her friends and fans remained dubious. And because the mind in doubt produces new monsters of its own, perhaps the question of how and why Mary Ure died on that particular night will never be answered to the satisfaction of everyone.

Chapter Eleven

MONSTER HOAXES

Nighttime in Anaheim, California, is the muffled sound of television sets booming in every house on the block, a dry west wind rustling in the tops of the eucalyptus trees and the distant hum of the traffic which never ceases rushing along in antlike frenzy on the busy Riverside Freeway that forms the northern edge of this sprawling Los Angeles suburb.

But nighttime in Anaheim for one woman in a quiet residential neighborhood not long ago meant taking the dog out for a quick turn of the backyard and glancing up suddenly to see a bright, eerie light in the sky.

A flying saucer! She'd read about them and heard about them. There could be no doubt—an alien space ship was hovering right over Anaheim. But this one was so big. And the strange, glowing light seemed to be surrounded by smaller lights. It must be a mother ship letting off all the other ships!

Leaving the bewildered dog to follow, she rushed into the kitchen and grabbed the telephone.

"What's the matter, Mom?" one of the kids said, but she waved the question away impatiently and dialed with a trembling forefinger. It took four rings to get an answer, they were always so slow. But finally there was a voice on the other end.

"Operator?" the woman panted. "Operator, this is an emergency! Get me the . . . the . . . oh, how do I know? Get me the fire department!"

It was an emergency all right. At least a 17-year-old neighbor thought so when the "huge flying saucer" was traced back to his modest hot-air balloon operation and the flimsy plastic dry-cleaning bag he had launched with cradle power from his own yard.

"I was trying to, well, scare people, and to see how long I could keep a balloon up," sheepishly admitted the youngster.

He spoke for a number of other California teenagers from San Diego to Los Angeles who for months had been enjoying the fad of scaring the daylights out

129

of anyone who chanced to glance up at the night sky.

Some of the kids used hot-air balloons pasted together out of tissue paper, but this particular boy, successful launcher of 100 balloons, was an expert. He usually used plastic bags such as clothes are draped in when they come from the cleaner, taping them shut at the top and attaching the bottom to a light wooden frame. Several candles stuck onto the frame provided plenty of heat to warm the air inside the bag to the point that it was lighter than the outside air. A wad of flaming paper was favored by some as a "take-off assist," but even with just the candles the balloons would begin their flight within seconds, sometimes climbing 1,000 feet and higher, and always casting a strange, eerie light.

A simple explanation? Sure. Simpler than jumping to the conclusion that one had seen a UFO? Of course. But although hot-air balloons have been around for hundreds of years, they're not particularly common these days; and many people fell for the more complicated notion that they'd seen a saucer.

Thus, the hoaxers of this world enjoyed yet another shout of merry laughter. They have been laughing for centuries, lavishly expending time, money and occasionally genius, plaguing science since science began. In fact, in the search for facts as to the controversial existence of monsters, pranksters have been so successful in leaving trails of fake evidence that skepticism about any given monster report is not wholly misplaced.

Some pranks are simple.

From the Pacific Coast comes the laughing confession of a man who enjoyed baffling Bigfoot hunters for several seasons by tromping around the woods wearing special shoes with big feet attached (although Bigfoot believers hotly claim that the hoaxer's tracks lacked the deep indentations characteristic of most

130

tracks. The real tracks, they say, could not possibly be made by any man or machine weighing less than 400 or 500 pounds, and, at that, a man or machine tall and agile enough to step over tall fences and skip over rough terrain).

From Georgia comes the claim of a truck driver that he ran over a "spaceman" with fatal results—fatal to the small, shriveled, faintly manlike creature whose body he exhibited as evidence. Police quickly discovered the body was that of a monkey which had been shaved bald and its tail cut off, but the story had gone out even quicker over a national wire service.

From Gulfport, Mississippi, down the coast from Pascagoula where the two fishermen swear they met saucer creatures, comes the report of a cabbie named Joseph Neely who said a blue light zipped down from the sky as he was driving along Highway 90, landed in front of his cab, caused his engine and his radio to die, and nearly causing him to do the same. "I ducked down in the seat," said Lane. "Then I heard a tapping sound on the windshield and looked up. I saw a horrible, flesh-colored creature with bright eyes and a crablike claw tapping on my window." He passed out.

It sounded like confirmation of the two fishermen's report—that is, until Neely confessed he had merely been napping on the job when a fellow cab driver caught him, and the imaginery fainting fit after an encounter with a spooky creature from outer space was the first excuse that popped into his mind.

Even Mother Nature plays pranks on us. According to one theory, she regularly provides us with dead sea serpents.

There was the Stronsa Beast that washed up on the Orkney Islands off the Scottish coast in 1808, and the huge carcass that washed up on a beach at Querqueville, France, in 1934, or, if you prefer a newer culmination for the centuries-old search for the Great

Sea Serpent, there was the massive creature whose rotting carcass was found on a beach at Scituate, Massachusetts, in November, 1970.

Nobody had ever seen anything like it. Witnesses were at a loss for words in trying to describe it. "It looked like a huge camel without legs," stammered one person who saw the thing. It had a long, thin neck, a small head, a thickish body with flippers and a long tail. Its weight was estimated at between 15 and 20 tons, and it was about 30 feet long.

Biologists rushed to the scene, and a great revelation was expected at any moment. But the revelation, when it came, was a small news item identifying the great Scituate Beast as merely another rotting carcass of a large basking shark, just like the Querqueville Beast and, it is inferred from descriptions, the Stronsa Beast.

It seems that the big, harmless monsters of the deep named basking sharks are unmistakably sharks when alive, but when one dies and the body begins to decompose, Nature plays her curious game of deception with us. The shark's gills fall away, carrying the jaws with it. Minus the gaping jaws of the shark, the species' most obvious feature has disappeared, leaving a tiny skull and a long spinal column that looks like a long neck. The lower part of the tail also falls away, and one sees an enormous blob vaguely resembling a legless camel. Thus, Mother Nature has her fun, and another candidate for the title of the Great Sea Serpent comes to the public attention.

Many jokes are not so harmless. Eminent professors still tell their classes about the fate of an Eighteenth-Century professor of natural philosophy named Johann Bartholomaeus Adam Beringer, who, in an early variation of the visitation-of-the-earth-by-godlike-powers theory, developed an odd hypothesis about fossils. "They are merely capricious fabrications of God," he

132

assured his classes, possibly hidden in the earth to test men's religious faith.

Day after day he droned about his theory, and his students at the University of Wurzburg, as students will, decided to play a joke on Beringer. They concocted ridiculous clay tablets bearing inscriptions in Hebrew, Babylonian, Syriac and Arabic and buried them here and there on a hillside where Beringer often took his students to seek geological specimens.

Professor Beringer was overjoyed at these "finds" which seemed to prove his pet theory. The students, elated by their success, next inscribed the signature of God Himself on one of their phony fossils.

With this proof in hand, Beringer promptly started writing elaborate scholarly descriptions in Latin of the fossils for a great book, and he had engravings made of the fossils at considerable expense.

The students decided they'd gone too far. They confessed to Professor Beringer. To their horror, he flatly refused to believe them and accused them of trying to rob him of the credit for his tremendous discovery.

His lengthy book appeared in 1728, to screams of helpless laughter from his colleagues in the scholarly world. Beringer's heart broke. He spent the remainder of his fortune trying to buy back all copies of his great work. It is said he died of a broken heart.

Similarly bogus "evidence" confused an entire generation of scholars attempting the difficult task of tracing back the family tree of man and apes (and, if you fancy the theory that they, too, are related, Bigfoot, the Abominable Snowman and their siblings). This is the famous hoax of Piltdown Man, whose fossil remains were supposedly unearthed in 1908 in England at Piltdown, Sussex, by an amateur archaeologist named Charles Dawson.

"He has found the missing link to prove Darwin's

133

theory of evolution," rhapsodized a London newspaper after Dawson turned over what looked like a large, human brain case and an apelike jaw to Britain's Museum of Natural History. Authorities concluded Dawson had unearthed the first evidence then available to science of a "dawn" man. Dawson was honored as a great discoverer until his death in 1916.

Oh, there were skeptics. And time and new scientific techniques proved they were right. By the 1950s, flourine age-dating tests provided the final piece in the puzzle, and the scholarly world went into shock. Someone—Dawson? a dentist?—had taken the jaw of an orangutan and skillfully ground down its teeth to make them look humanlike, then had stained the orang's jaw and a modern man's cranium to try to disguise the fact that they were (1) not between 200,-000 and a million years old, as had originally been thought, and (2) not at all from the same creature.

Science, which had been faked out all those years by a clever hoax, finally was able to correct the human sequence of evolution by kicking out the greatest anomaly in the fossil record.

And the pranksters are still working hard at creating famous pranks. One marvelous hoax entered the annals of non-science nonsense in December, 1968 under the name of The Iceman when zoologists Ivan T. Sanderson and Bernard Heuvelmans skidded and plowed their way into the snowbound yard of a remote farm in Minnesota to inspect a creature first stated to have been found floating in a 6,000-pound block of natural ice in the Sea of Okhotsk in Siberia.

Sanderson had tracked the creature down after being tipped off that it was being kept on the farm by Frank D. Hansen following a two-year carnival tour.

It was December 17th when Sanderson and Heuvelmans arrived at Hansen's farm. There was more snow coming down, and the two zoologists shivered as they were led not to a roaring fire, but to a cold trailer. There, in a refrigerated coffin, in a thick sheath of ice, lay a large, hairy creature with flaring nostrils, a slitlike mouth and big eye-sockets staring emptily through the eternal ice.

Sanderson and Heuvelmans were both wary, but two days of study were so convincing to Heuvelmans that he named it on the spot, *Homo pongoide,* and contended to the scientific world that an unknown species of man, apparently related to Neanderthal Man, had been found.

His examination was somewhat handicapped, of course, by the exhibitor's insistence that he was unable to thaw the giant creature out.

Soon the plot thickened. A young damsel named Helen Westring published a story claiming that while on a hunting trip all by herself in the snowy woods of Minnesota, she met an Abominable Snowman. She shot it through the right eye, and The Iceman died, presumably thereafter to be frozen in its block of ice. The exhibitor then changed his pace and published a story claiming that instead of the creature's having been found in Siberia, *he* shot it in the woods of Minnesota, became panicked when he discovered it was manlike and stuck it in his wife's deep-freeze for seven years before unveiling it first to the world of carnivals, then science.

Bigfoot lovers had a field day throughout the entire Iceman affair. The FBI was asked to investigate bullet holes in this creature which had been called humanoid to see if murder charges should be filed (it refused jurisdiction). The august Smithsonian Institute, asked at one point to examine The Iceman, publicly announced its disinterest.

At last word, the "genuine" corpse had disappeared, and only a substitute monster made of latex by a West Coast firm lived on.

So when the accusation of "Hoax!" rings out on the

135

heels of a reported monster, as it does repeatedly, keep in mind that skeptics often have reason for their skepticism.

And if you yourself chance to see something strange —an eerie light glowing in the sky?—also give a thought to the scientific principle called Occam's razor.

The principle of Occam's razor means, in brief, that if two or more explanations will solve a puzzle, you ought to consider first the simpler explanation. For example, that eerie light could be an invasion of flying saucers. But it might also be just a plain old plastic dry-cleaner's bag launched with two candles by a laughing neighbor kid.

Chapter Twelve

A NEED FOR MONSTERS

Reports of monsters are universals of time and space, and a fascination with monsters from Grendel to the Jolly Green Giant is characteristic of all human societies.

Why?

A striking feature of the affluent, post-World War Two society has been an increased hunger for horror, leading to a boom in scary movies and to the concomitant impulse that encourages modern kids to munch Count Chocula and Frankenberry cereals for breakfast, swallow their monster vitamins, then rush off to play with their very own "Mad Monster" Dracula dolls in their Mad Monster Castles.

Why?

Serious, sensible people report month after month that they have seen large, hairy creatures striding through deep woods, or have been run off the highway by a primeval monster with batlike wings, or have seen an enormous, coiling mass thrashing through the still waters of Loch Ness or Lake Champlain.

Why?

Psychologists we have consulted say that people need their monsters, whether they seriously believe in the existence of monsters or simply enjoy the two hundredth rerun of "King Kong" on the late, late show, and that monsters provide useful props for working through dark impulses that still course through the subterranean passages of the human psyche.

According to one West Coast psychologist, Dr. Douglas M. Cairns, people who are partial to monsters can be generally categorized, for instance, as the thrill seeker, or the person who is attempting to deal either with anxiety or destructive impulses. Here's how a brief sampling of the categories work:

The thrill seeker seeks excitement or variety in his life. Dr. Cairns says this person feels that his own life lacks color and seeks to enjoy vicariously the conquests and pursuits of the monster. He likes to go to a movie or read a book and be scared.

The anxious individual, on the other hand, may feel many free-floating fears and anxieties which he can't easily control, and enjoys reading the monster book or watching the monster film where there are build-ups of tension and anxiety that he *can* control. This gives him satisfaction, since in reading or viewing, he knows he can simply turn away from the screen or close the book if he starts feeling uncomfortable. He has control over his fears.

"On another level of analysis," says Dr. Cairns, "is the person who has a fascination for the destructive monsters—the monster who devoured Cleveland, killing a million people. This individual may have many destructive impulses, and since he cannot deal with these in a socially acceptable manner, he finds that watching monsters destroy people and things may

137

give him satisfaction. Therefore, it is seen in terms of sublimation of destructiveness."

When it comes down to people who actually believe they've seen a UFO or a Mothman with a 10-foot wingspan flapping through the skies, Dr. Cairns points out that monsters can come out of our social relationships, as well as our ids.

If your best friend is thoroughly convinced that flying saucers are making terrestrial landings, willynilly you're apt to develop an interest in flying saucers too, just from being around him and listening to him talk. You might scoff at first, but once your interest develops, you might as well start going with him to gatherings where a lot of other people believe in and talk about UFOs. You could end up as a believer. It's sort of like turning around the statement, "I go to church because I'm religious," and saying, "I'm religious because I go to church."

The non-believer in monsters who strolls sleepily on his back porch one night and suddenly thinks, "Ye gads, I see a Sasquatch!" is not immune from society's in-put, either. If he has read or heard of similar monster sightings—and who hasn't?—it's easy enough for the mind to convert a dark shadow into a real monster, because people tend to "see" what they are looking for.

There's an element of wishful thinking too, according to Wayne Suttles, a professor of anthropology at Portland State University, who has put it this way:

"When we were little kids, we learned about strange creatures and monsters, and then as we grew up, we learned that they weren't real, that we had to give them up. When we 'find' one again, it's like finding your Teddy bear in the attic."

But nothing irritates the true believer more than science's ability to find rational alternatives for explaining away his beliefs. People who are absolutely,

138

genuinely convinced that they have seen some strange being up to strange tricks lament that scientists merely ignore their reports, and some become so exasperated that they go in for the old "conspiracy" theory—the one that runs, "Scientists deliberately conceal all evidence that might prove upsetting to their own pet theories."

However, it's more plausible to believe in the existence of monsters than it is to believe in the conspiracy idea, for there is at least soft evidence available to back up the former theory, and far less evidence at all for the latter.

It is true, though, that science often ignores monster reports. It is also true that there is a reason for it. Given adequate evidence, science can prove that something *does* exist, but proving the non-existence of anything is extremely hard, if not logically impossible.

So science waits for the hard evidence on the existence of monsters to come in, and the rest of us are left to decide for ourselves—by pondering each season's news items, by weighing the reports that other scholars pick up and repeat in their books and articles, and perhaps by wondering if our eyes and ears deceive us if we chance to see a strange footprint or hear a sudden bestial cry in the night.

The wait for the final truth cannot be a long one. In this shrinking world in which our encroachment on the last wildernesses is forcing rare and endangered species of animals into a race for their lives, species of monsters, if they exist, will either be crowded out into the public eye or they, too, will become extinct.

Or we will invent new ones.

A NOTE TO READERS

If the subject of monsters intrigues you, you may wish to do more reading on the subject. The following is a selected list of books which offers a wide spectrum of information and opinion. Some we cannot honestly recommend as offering a thoughtful, rational approach, but they are fascinating. While emphasis is placed on recent publications, some older books have been included because of their continuing interest.

BIBLIOGRAPHY

Berlitz, Charles. *Bermuda Triangle*. New York: Doubleday & Company, Inc., 1974.

Bernstein, Morey. *The Search for Bridey Murphy*. New York: Doubleday & Company, Inc., 1965 (revised edition).

Binder, Otto. *Unsolved Mysteries of the Past*. New York: Tower Publications, Inc.

Blum, Ralph and Judy. *Beyond Earth: Man's Contact with UFOs*. New York: Bantam Books, Inc., 1974.

Blumrich, Josef F. *The Spaceships of Ezekiel*. New York: Bantam Books, Inc., 1974.

Brown, Charles Edward. *Sea Serpents: Wisconsin Occurrences of these Weird Watery Monsters*. Madison: Wisconsin Folklore Society, 1942.

Brown, Raymond Lamont. *A Book of Witchcraft*. New York: Taplinger Publishing Company, Inc., 1971.

Condon, Edward U. *Scientific Study of Unidentified Flying Objects*. New York: Bantam Books, Inc., 1969.

Costello, Peter. *In Search of Lake Monsters*. New York: Coward, McCann & Geoghegan, 1974.

Edwards, Frank. *Strange World*. New York: Lyle Stuart, Inc., 1964.

Emenegger, Robert. *UFO's, Past, Present & Future*. New York: Ballantine Books, 1974.

Fuller, John G. *Incident at Exeter*. New York: G. P. Putnam's Sons, 1966.

Godwin, John. *This Baffling World*. New York: Hart Publishing Company, 1968.

Green, John. *On the Track of the Sasquatch*. Agassiz, B.C.: Cheam Publications Ltd., 1968.

———. *The Year of the Sasquatch*. Agassiz, B.C.: Cheam Publications Ltd., 1970.

Greenhouse, Herbert B. *The Book of Psychic Knowledge*. New York: Taplinger Publishing Company, Inc., 1973.

Grumley, Michael. *There Are Giants in the Earth*. New York: Doubleday & Company, Inc., 1974.

Heuvelmans, Bernard. *On the Track of Unknown Animals*. New York: Hill & Wang, 1965.

Hill, Douglas and Pat Williams. *The Supernatural*. London: Aldus Books Limited, 1965.

Hynek, J. Allen. *The UFO Experiences: A Scientific Inquiry*. Chicago: Henry Regnery Co., 1972.

Janus, Christopher G., with William Brashler. *The Search for Peking Man*. New York: Macmillan, 1975

Keel, John A. *The Mothman Prophecies*. New York: Saturday Review Press, 1975.

———. *Our Haunted Planet*. Greenwich: Fawcett Publications, 1971.

———. *UFOs: Operation Trojan Horse*. New York: G.P. Putnam's Sons, 1970.

Keyhoe, Donald E. *Aliens from Space: The Real Story of Unidentified Flying Objects*. New York: Doubleday & Company, Inc., 1973.

Landsburg, Alan and Sally. *In Search of Ancient Mysteries*. New York: Bantam Books, Inc., 1974.

Laycock, George. *Strange Monsters & Great Searches*. New York: Doubleday & Company, Inc., 1973.

McWane, Glenn and David Graham. *The New UFO Sightings*. New York: Warner Books, Inc., 1974.

Millar, Ronald. *Piltdown Men*. New York: Ballantine Books.

Napier, John. *Bigfoot*. New York: E. P. Dutton & Co., Inc., 1973.

Nichols, Elizabeth. *The Devil's Sea*. New York: Award Books, 1975.

Norman, Eric. *Gods, Demons and Space Chariots*. New York: Lancer Books, Inc., 1970.

Sagan, Carl. *Other Worlds*. New York: Bantam Books, Inc., 1975.

————. *The Cosmic Connection*. New York: Doubleday & Company, Inc., 1973.

Sanderson, Ivan T. *Abominable Snowman: Legend Come to Life*. New York: Chilton Co., 1961.

Sendy, Jean. *The Coming of the Gods*. New York: Berkeley Publishing Co., 1970.

Shapiro, Harry L. *Peking Man*. New York: Simon & Schuster, 1975.

Sherman, Harold. *ESP*. New York: World Publishing Co., 1969.

Spencer, John Wallace. *Limbo of the Lost*. Westfield, Mass.: Phillips Publishing Co., 1973.

Spraggett, Allen. *The World of the Unexplained*. New York: New American Library, 1974.

Tchernine, Odette. *The Yeti*. London: Neville Spearman, 1970.

Ullman, James Ramsey, with Tenzing Norgay. *Tiger of the Snows*. New York: G. P. Putnam's Sons, 1955.

Vallee, Jacques. *Anatomy of a Phenomenon: UFO's in Space*. Chicago: Henry Regnery Co., 1965.

Von Däniken, Erich. *Chariots of the Gods?* New York: G. P. Putnam's Sons, 1970.

Whyte, Constance. *The Loch Ness Monster*. Inverness, 1951.

Wilson, Clifford. *UFOs and Their Mission Impossible*. New York: New American Library, 1975.

Winer, Richard. *The Devil's Triangle*. New York: Bantam Books, Inc., 1974.